AN INTRODUCTION TO
THE SINGAPORE LEGAL SYSTEM

Written for the ASEAN Law Association

by

HELENA H.M. CHAN, LL.B. (Hons.) (Sing.), LL.M. (Harv.),
Advocate and Solicitor of the Supreme Court, Singapore
Lecturer, Faculty of Law,
National University of Singapore.

SINGAPORE
MALAYAN LAW JOURNAL PTE. LTD.
1986

UNITED KINGDOM
Sweet & Maxwell Ltd.
London

AUSTRALIA
The Law Book Company Limited
Sydney: Melbourne: Brisbane

©
HELENA H.M. CHAN
MALAYAN LAW JOURNAL PTE. LTD.
1986

All rights reserved. No part of this publication may be reproduced or transmitted, in any form or by any means, including electronic, mechanical, photocopying and recording, without the written permission of the copyright holder, application for which should be addressed to the publisher. Such written permission must be obtained before any part of this publication is stored in a retrieval system of any nature.

Published in 1986 by
MALAYAN LAW JOURNAL PTE. LTD.
3 Shenton Way #14-03, Shenton House, Singapore 0106;
Typeset and printed by Eurasia Press, Singapore

ISBN 9971-70-054-9

To my parents

Preface

This book is not a treatise on the Singapore legal system. Rather, it is intended as a short general introduction to the Singapore legal system for the law student, foreign lawyer or interested layman wanting an overview of the salient features of the legal system of Singapore. The book is divided into six chapters. Chapter I traces Singapore's legal history and how she came to be part of the English common law family. Chapter II goes on to examine the sources of Singapore law, and Chapter III sketches out the state structure within which the Singapore legal system operates. Chapter IV examines the key legal institutions in the country, *i.e.*, the judicial system, the legal profession, the Legal Service, the Attorney-General and some of the major law enforcement agencies. Chapter V takes a look at procedure and outlines the various phases of civil and criminal proceedings. The book concludes with some brief observations on the legal culture of Singapore and a few tentative comments on her future legal development.

Bearing in mind the somewhat varied audience for which this book was written, I have attempted, in some parts, to go beyond a purely descriptive approach in the belief that historical and comparative information would make the account more interesting and meaningful. Also, in order to cater to law students and foreign lawyers, certain topics (*e.g.* procedure) have been covered in possibly more technical detail than might interest the layman reader. The limitations and problems inherent in a work of this nature are obvious. There were problems in determining the precise topics and details to be covered, bearing in mind the diversity of the audience and the desire to present as accurate a picture of the Singapore legal system as is possible to do in a nutshell. It is the writer's hope that, in spite of the many blemishes that undoubtedly exist, this objective has been substantially accomplished.

I would like to express my deepest gratitude: to Associate Professor (Mrs.) Tan Sook Yee, Dean, Faculty of Law, National University of Singapore, for encouraging me to take on the project of writing this book for the Asean Law Association; to Tun Mohamed Suffian, Immediate Past President of the Asean Law Association, for his enthusiastic support; to my friends, Andrew Phang Boon Leong, Wong Meng Yeng and Yeo Hwee Ying for taking time off their busy schedules to make comments and suggestions on the manuscript; and lastly, but not least of all, to my publishers, for their patience and assistance. Needless to say, all errors and imperfections herein remain the writer's sole responsibility.

I have attempted to state the law as at 31 March 1986.

HELENA H.M. CHAN

Singapore
April, 1986

Table of Contents

Preface v
Abbreviations viii

Chapter I.   Legal History 1
                 A. A Brief Outline of Political History 1
                 B. The General Reception of English Law 4
                 C. Specific Reception of English Law 14
                 D. Other Legal Influences 19

Chapter II.   Sources of Law 21
                 A. The Constitution 21
                 B. Statutes 23
                 C. Subsidiary Legislation 26
                 D. Judicial Precedents 28
                 E. Custom 39

Chapter III.   The Structure of Government 41
                 A. The Executive 41
                 B. The Legislature 43
                 C. The Judiciary 48

Chapter IV.   Legal Institutions 49
                 A. The Judicial System 49
                 B. The Legal Profession 80
                 C. The Legal Service 92
                 D. The Attorney-General 94
                 E. Major Law Enforcement Agencies 96

Chapter V.   Procedure 102
                 A. General 102
                 B. Criminal Procedure 107
                 C. Civil Procedure 119

Chapter VI.   Conclusion 130
                 A. Legal Culture 130
                 B. Future Legal Development 134

Index 139

Abbreviations

The abbreviations more frequently encountered in the book are listed here for convenient reference.

A.C.	Appeal Cases (United Kingdom)
All E.R.	All England Law Reports (United Kingdom)
A.M.L.A.	Administration of Muslim Law Act, Cap. 42
Art.	Article (of the Reprint of the Constitution of the Republic of Singapore 1980)
Cap.	Chapter (of Singapore Statutes, Revised Edition 1970)
C.P.C.	Criminal Procedure Code, Reprint 1980 (Cap. 113)
G.N.	Gazette Notification
Ky.	Kyshe's Law Reports
L.P.A.	Legal Profession Act, Reprint 1982 (Cap. 217)
M.L.J.	Malayan Law Journal
Mal. L.R.	Malaya Law Review
Ord.	Order
r(r).	rule(s)
R.S.C.	Rules of the Supreme Court 1970
s(s).	section (s)
S.C.A.	Subordinate Courts Act, Cap. 14
S.C.J.A.	Supreme Court of Judicature Act, Cap. 15
S.C.R.	Subordinate Courts Rules 1986
S.C.T.A.	Small Claims Tribunals Act 1984, No. 27 of 1984
W.L.R.	Weekly Law Reports (United Kingdom)

Chapter I

Legal History

The Singapore legal system belongs to the English common law family. This means that in terms of methodology, the style of legal thought and reasoning, the structure of legal institutions, the doctrines of legal classification and procedure, the Singapore legal system bears a close resemblance to the English legal system. A newcomer to South-East Asia might well wonder how it came about that Singapore and her close neighbours, Malaysia and Brunei, belong to the common law family, when other countries in the same region (*e.g.* Thailand and Indonesia) are part of the civil law family. The short answer, of course, is colonisation or influence by different western powers during the colonial era. Thus, for example, Dutch colonisation was responsible for bringing Indonesia into the civil law fold, whereas British colonisation was the reason Singapore, Malaysia and Brunei became part of the common law family.

In order to understand the contemporary Singapore legal system, it is first necessary to understand its historical roots, which are closely intertwined with those of the neighbouring Malaysian legal system. However, before we delve into the legal history of Singapore, it would be helpful to begin with a brief sketch of the political history of Singapore[1] and the Malay peninsula as this would facilitate a better understanding of Singapore legal history.[2]

A. A Brief Outline of Political History

British colonisation of the Malay peninsula began in the late eighteenth century.[3] The story opened in 1786, when the English East India Company, spurred on by Dutch competition and the need for a strategic port on the Straits of Malacca to shelter their India-China trade, succeeded in acquiring the virtually uninhabited island of

---

[1] For a brief overview of Singapore's political history from the thirteenth century to the modern day, see Singapore *1985*, pp. 44-54, 65-66.
[2] This will also give the reader a better appreciation of the problems of *stare decisis* in Singapore today: see *infra*, Chapter II.D.
[3] There is an abundance of literature on this topic: see e.g. J.F. Cady, *Southeast Asia: Its Historical Development* (1964), pp. 309-310, 320-322; D.G.E. Hall, *A History of South-East Asia* (3rd ed. 1970), pp. 489-501; L.A Mills, *British Malaya 1824-67* (1961), pp. 30-59; K.G. Tregonning, *The British in Malaya: The First Forty Years 1786-1826* (1965).

Penang from the Sultan of Kedah.[4] In 1795, the British occupied Dutch Malacca, but restored it to the Dutch in 1818 under the Treaty of Vienna of 1814. However, British occupation of Malacca had made them realise the strategic importance to British trade of having a station that commanded the Malacca Straits.[5] Anxiety over losing Malacca led the British to Singapore in 1819.[6] At that time, Singapore was virtually uninhabited except for some 150 Malay fishermen under the authority of the Temenggong who was an official of the Johore Sultanate.[7] There were also some Chinese inhabitants.[8] The East India Company, under a treaty of friendship and alliance concluded with the Temenggong, obtained permission to establish a trading post on the island. In 1824, the Sultan of Johore ceded Singapore to the British. The East India Company thereby acquired full sovereignty in perpetuity over Singapore. In the same year, Malacca was ceded to the British under the Anglo-Dutch Treaty of 1824.

Thus, by 1824, the English East India Company was in possession of three settlements in the Malay peninsula — Penang, Malacca and Singapore. Penang had been made a separate Presidency in 1805.[9] In 1824, Malacca and Singapore were placed under the Bengal Presidency.[10] In 1826, an English Act of Parliament[11] detached Singapore and Malacca from the Bengal Presidency and united them with Penang to form the separate Presidency of the Straits Settlements.[12] However, in 1830, the Straits Settlements ceased to have a separate government and became subject to the Presidency of Bengal.[13] With Singapore as the administrative centre, the Straits Settlements remained for the most part under the India Office till 1867,[14] when mounting dissatisfaction with Indian administration

---

[4] See W.J. Napier, *An Introduction to the Study of the Law Administered in the Colony of the Straits Settlements* (1898), pp. 1-2.
[5] *One Hundred Years of Singapore: Vol. 1*, (W. Makepeace, G. Brooke & R. Braddell eds. 1921), p. 20; see also Hall, *supra*, n. 3 at p. 500.
[6] See Napier, *supra*, n. 4 at pp. 8-9; Hall, *supra*, n. 3 at pp. 499-501.
[7] See Mills, *supra*, n. 3 at p. 68.
[8] See W. Bartley, "The Population of Singapore in 1819" in *Singapore: 150 Years*, MBRAS Reprint No. 1 (1973), p. 117.
[9] See Napier, *supra*, n. 4 at p. 6.
[10] *Id.*, at p. 11.
[11] 6 Geo. IV. c. 85.
[12] *Supra*, n. 10.
[13] *Id.*
[14] See Napier, *supra*, n. 4 at p. 13; R. Braddell, *The Law of the Straits Settlements: A Commentary* (3rd ed. 1982), pp. 38-39.

Legal History 3

climaxed in the transfer of the Straits Settlements to the direct control of the Colonial Office in London.[15] The Straits Settlements (together with Labuan which had been acquired in 1846) thereby became a Crown Colony and remained so until 1946.

British influence, in the meantime, had also been extending beyond the Straits Settlements. By 1888, Sarawak and North Borneo had become protected states.[16] In 1896, the four protected Malay sultanates of Negri Sembilan, Pahang, Perak and Selangor were brought together to form a loose federation called the Federated Malay States (*i.e.*, the F.M.S.). The remaining five Malay states (*i.e.*, Johore, Kedah, Kelantan, Perlis and Trengganu) were conveniently referred to as the unfederated Malay states (*i.e.*, the U.F.M.S.), and although they subsequently accepted British protection, they did not join the former group.[17]

From 1942 to 1945, British Malaya was occupied by the Japanese. After the Japanese surrender, the British resumed control. However, the war had been instrumental in fanning the flame of nationalism in European colonies throughout the region.[18] The movement for independence gathered momentum after the war ended.

In Malaya, the post-war period was marked by much political turmoil. With the return of the British, political reorganisation took place to prepare British Malaya for future independence. In 1946, the Straits Settlements were disbanded. Singapore became a separate Crown colony whilst Penang, Malacca, the F.M.S. and the U.F.M.S. were united to form the Malayan Union.[19] In the same year, Sarawak and North Borneo became British colonies by cession.[20] The short-lived Malayan Union was replaced by the Federation of Malaya in 1948.[21] In the same year, the Malayan Communist Party launched an

---

[15] See Hall, *supra*, n. 3 at p. 520.
[16] K.G. Tregonning, *A History of Modern Malaysia and Singapore* (Rev. 2nd ed. 1972), pp. 249-250.
[17] See J.M. Gullick, *Malaya* (1963), pp. 35-36. For an account of the historical reasons behind British expansion in peninsular Malaya, see Cady, *supra*, n. 3 at pp. 435, 443-445; D.R. SarDesai, *British Trade and Expansion in Southeast Asia: 1830-1914* (1977), pp. 140-176; *Malaya: The Making of a Neo-Colony* (M. Amin and M. Caldwell eds. 1977), pp. 13-37.
[18] See Cady, *supra*, n. 3 at p. 584.
[19] See C.M. Turnbull, *A History of Singapore: 1819-1975* (1977), pp. 220-230.
[20] See Tregonning, *supra*, n. 16 at pp. 250, 255.
[21] *Id.*, at pp. 230-232.

"armed struggle" to overthrow the government. The "Emergency," as this episode in Malayan history came to be called, engaged British, Commonwealth and Malayan security forces for 12 years before it was finally declared at an end in 1960.[22]

In 1957, under the Federation of Malaya Agreement, "Merdeka" (*i.e.*, Independence) was proclaimed, and the Federation of Malaya became a sovereign state within the British Commonwealth. As for Singapore, internal self-government was finally won in 1959, and the colony became the State of Singapore.[23] In 1963, the merger of Singapore, Sarawak, North Borneo and the Federation of Malaya created the Federation of Malaysia.[24] Singapore's membership of this union was very brief. In 1965, political differences[25] climaxed in her secession. Since then, Singapore has been an independent republic.

Against this backdrop of political history, we can begin to trace Singapore's legal history and development.

B. The General Reception of English Law

For the first twenty years after the English East India Company acquired Penang in 1786, legal chaos prevailed on the island.[26] No known body of law was administered. The company's officers administered justice according to the dictates of their conscience, administering Malay and Chinese law to the local inhabitants, but having no power over Europeans and British subjects.[27] To remedy this situation, the Crown, in 1807, granted the East India Company the First Charter of Justice, which set up a Court of Judicature in Penang. This court was to have the jurisdiction and powers of English superior courts so far as circumstances admitted,[28] and was to pass judgment according to "justice and right."[29] Appeals therefrom lay directly to the King in Council[30] (*i.e.*, the Privy Council).

---

[22] See Gullick, *supra*, n. 17 at pp. 96-108.
[23] See Turnbull, *supra*, n. 19 at pp. 267-270.
[24] See Tregonning, *supra*, n. 16 at pp. 258-272.
[25] For more details, see *Singapore: An Illustrated History: 1941-1984* (Information Division, Ministry of Culture, Singapore, 1984), pp. 266-270; S.S. Bedlington, *Malaysia and Singapore — The Building of New States* (1978), pp. 207-209; Tregonning, *supra*, n. 16 at pp. 273-276; Turnbull, *supra*, n. 19, at pp. 286-293.
[26] Napier, *supra*, n. 4.
[27] Braddell, *supra*, n. 14 at pp. 6-8.
[28] *Id.*, at p. 12.
[29] *Id.*, at p. 13.
[30] *Id.*

Legal History 5

The same legal chaos prevailed in Singapore[31] till 1826 when the Second Charter of Justice was granted on the petition of the East India Company. This Charter abolished the old court (which had served only Penang) and created a new one to serve Penang, Singapore and Malacca. By 1855, Singapore had developed so rapidly that it was felt necessary to reorganise the existing court structure to provide for a separate division with its own recorder, serving just Singapore and Malacca. This was done by the Third Charter of Justice.[32]

The wording of these three Charters is essentially the same[33]; and it may generally be said that they had as their main object, the establishment of proper courts on the English model for the orderly administration of justice.

Once a proper judicial system was set up, the first matter that had to be determined was this: what law was the new court to apply?

The Charters themselves were vague and contained no express direction on this point beyond conferring on the court the jurisdiction and powers of English courts, and directing it to pass judgment according to "justice and right." The Charters did not declare *"totidem verbis* that ... [the law of England was to] ... be the territorial law of the Island."[34] The effect of the Charters has never been ruled upon by the Privy Council.[35]

Nevertheless, the colonial judges unanimously decided that the First Charter of 1807 (which applied only to Penang) introduced English law as it then stood, into Penang.[36] Similarly, in the case of the Second Charter of Justice of 27 November 1826 (which extended the jurisdiction of the existing court to cover Singapore and Malacca), a string of decisions from 1835 to 1890 held that English law as it existed on 27 November 1826, was introduced into the Straits Settlements by this Charter.[37] There are apparently no further cases on this point, but the position has long been regarded as being settled

---

[31] Napier, *supra*, n. 4 at p. 10; Braddell, *supra*, n. 14 at p. 23.
[32] Braddell, *supra*, n. 14 at p. 34.
[33] *Id.*, at pp. 27 and 34.
[34] Sir Benson Maxwell R. in *R. v. Willans* (1858) 3 Ky. 16 at 25.
[35] Braddell, *supra*, n. 14 at pp. 14 and 27; Napier, *supra*, n. 4 at pp. 21-22.
[36] Braddell, *supra*, n. 14 at p. 14; Napier, *supra*, n. 4 at p. 21.
[37] Braddell, *supra*, n. 14 at pp. 27-29; Napier, *supra*, n. 4 at p. 22.

beyond any serious dispute.[38] Thus, in the celebrated case of *Regina v. Willans*, Sir Benson Maxwell expressed the consensus of local judicial opinion when he said that "a direction in an English Charter to decide according to justice and right, without expressly stating by what known body of law they shall be dispensed and so to decide in a country which has not already an established body of law, is plainly a direction to decide according to the law of England."[39]

However, the Third Charter of Justice of 1855 was not regarded as effecting a re-introduction of English law as it stood at that date, because, as opposed to the Second Charter which created a new court, the Third Charter merely reorganised the structure of the existing court.[40]

Therefore, as a result of the Second Charter of Justice of 1826, Singapore received a court system on the prevailing English model, and as a result of judicial interpretation of the language of the Second Charter, it was generally accepted that the law of England as it stood on 27 November 1826 was received into Singapore.[41] The latter phenomenon is commonly referred to as "the general reception of English law." In these two ways, the foundations of the nascent Singapore legal system were firmly laid in the English common law family.[42]

Having decided that the Second Charter of Justice had the effect of introducing pre-1826 English law into the Straits Settlements, the colonial judges had to grapple with yet another problem. From the very beginning, consistent with earlier British colonial practice elsewhere,[43] it was recognised that the general reception of English

---

[38] Braddell, *supra*, n. 14 at p. 29; L.A. Sheridan, *The British Commonwealth: Vol. 9: Malaya and Singapore, The Borneo Territories* (1961), p. 14. *cf.* Mohan Gopal, "English Law in Singapore: The Reception That Never Was" [1983] 1 M.L.J. xxv.

[39] (1858) 3 Ky. 16 at 25.

[40] Sir Benson Maxwell R. in *Regina v. Willans* (1858) 3 Ky. 16 at 37; Braddell, *supra*, n. 14 at pp. 34-35.

[41] See G.W. Bartholomew, "Introduction" in *Tables of the Written Laws of the Republic of Singapore: 1819-1971: Vol. 1 — Local Legislation* (compiled by E. Srinivasagam and staff of the Law Library, University of Singapore, 1972), pp. xix-xx. It is interesting to note that a similar development took place in British India: see M.C. Setalvad, *The Common Law in India* (1960), p. 23; B.N. Pandey, *The Introduction of English Law into India* (1967), p. 37.

[42] See G.W. Bartholomew, "The Singapore Legal System" in *Singapore: Society in Transition* (Riaz Hassan, ed. 1976), p. 89.

[43] For example, in the American colonies: see K. Zweigert & H. Kotz, *An Introduction to Comparative Law: Vol. I* (1977), pp. 245-246; R. David & J. Brierley, *Major Legal Systems in the World Today* (3rd ed. 1985), pp. 398-400.

law under the Second Charter was not a "blanket" reception of the entire body of English law as it stood on 27 November 1826[44] because not all English laws were suitable for application in the Straits Settlements. The problem then was this: what qualifications should be made to the general reception of English law? Which English laws should be received into the Straits Settlements? When should they be modified, and if so, to what extent?

The Charters, common law and imperial practice provided no precise guidelines for tackling this problem. The task of clarifying the qualifications to general reception and deciding which English laws were received and which were not, fell mainly to the colonial courts in the first instance,[45] and ultimately, to the Privy Council as court of last resort for Britain's overseas empire. This task was by no means simple, for, as Lord Cranworth lamented in 1858:

> Nothing is more difficult than to know which of our laws is to be regarded as imported into our colonies ... Who is to decide whether they are adopted or not? That is a very difficult question.[46]

Nevertheless, over a period of time, a series of judicial decisions gradually established that the general reception of English law in the Straits Settlements under the Second Charter was subject to three qualifications. To begin with, only English law of general policy and application was to be received.[47] Further, such English law was to be applied subject to local customs and religions, and local legislation. Since this is still the position in Singapore today, each of these qualifications to general reception will now be examined in greater detail.

1. Only English Law of General Policy and Application is Received

In *Yeap Cheah Neo* v. *Ong Cheong Neo*, an appeal from the Straits Settlement of Penang, the Privy Council said that "statutes relating to matters and exigencies peculiar to the local condition of England, and

---

[44] Bartholomew, *supra*, n. 42 at p. 90.
[45] See *e.g. Syed Ali bin Mohamed Alsagoff* v. *Syed Omar bin Mohamed Alsagoff* (1918) 15 S.S.L.R. 103, in which the Court of Appeal of the Straits Settlements had to determine the applicability of the rule against perpetuities as embodied in *Whitby* v. *Mitchell* (1889-1890) 44 Ch. D. 85.
[46] *Whicker* v. *Hume* 11 E.R. 50, H.L. at 65.
[47] Sir Benson Maxwell, C.J. in *Choa Choon Neo* v. *Spottiswoode* (1869) 12 Ky. 216 at 221.

which are not adapted to the circumstances of a particular Colony, do not become a part of its law, although the general law of England may be introduced into it."[48] On this test, their lordships approved the exclusion of English statutes relating to superstitious uses[49] and mortmain.[50] However, they upheld the introduction of the rule against perpetuities,[51] reasoning that the policy behind it (*i.e.*, ensuring free alienability of land) was as desirable in Penang as it was in England.

Thus, for a pre-1826 English law to be potentially applicable in Singapore, it has, in the first place, to be of general application *i.e.*, suitable to Singapore.

2. English Law that is Received will be Applied So Far As the Several Religions, Manners and Customs of the Inhabitants will Admit.[52]

Even where an English law was generally applicable, it might theoretically have to undergo modified application so as not to work injustice and oppression on the local population.[53] The question of how far native law and customs were to be given effect perplexed colonial courts initially because, unlike their Indian counterparts, the three Charters contained no express provision for the administration of native law to native races.[54] Therefore, the preliminary question was whether English law should, as a matter of principle, be modified to accommodate local custom.

The earliest opinions favoured giving the local population the full benefit of their own laws, religions and customs.[55] An extreme exam-

---

[48] (1875) L.R. 6 P.C. 381 at 394.
[49] *I.e.*, trusts which have for their object the propagation of the rites of a religion not tolerated by the law, and which are therefore void: See R. Bird, *Osborn's Concise Law Dictionary* (7th ed. 1983), p. 316.
[50] *I.e.*, the alienation of land to corporations, whereby the benefit of the incidents of tenure was lost, because "a corporation never dies": *id.*, p. 225.
[51] This rule prohibits any disposition of property which postpones or may postpone the absolute vesting of such property beyond the period of the life or lives of any number of persons living at the time of the disposition, and the further period of 21 years after the death of the survivor, with the possible addition of the period of gestation. Perpetuities are contrary to the policy of the law because they "tie up" property and prevent its free alienation: *id*, p. 251.
[52] *Supra*, n. 47.
[53] *Id.*; approved by the Privy Council in *Yeap Cheah Neo* v. *Ong Cheng Neo* (1875) at 394-397, and *Khoo Hooi Leong* v. *Khoo Chong Yeok* [1930] A.C. 346.
[54] Braddell, *supra*, n. 14 at p. 79.
[55] *Id.*

ple of this is seen in the only recorded decision under the First Charter on this point, in which the third Recorder, Sir Ralph Rice, expressed his view that the Charter imported only English criminal law into Penang, and that civil matters were governed by native law and customs.[56] As late as 1857, in the first reported case under the Third Charter, Sir Richard McClausland, R., opined that it was "the policy of the framers of the Charter to induce as many persons as possible to become resident in the Settlement and not to interfere with the observance of their several religions, manners and customs, nor with the free disposition of their houses, lands, or moveable property."[57]

The following year, Sir Benson Maxwell, in the celebrated case of *Regina* v. *Willans*, swung to the other extreme by denying that the Charter had authorised the modification of English law to accommodate local custom and usage.[58] However, the contrary view eventually prevailed in the local courts and was endorsed by three Privy Council decisions which made it clear that the courts were willing to modify the application of English law to prevent the injustice or oppression that would otherwise result.[59] Thus, for example, the Privy Council affirmed the local judiciary's recognition of Chinese polygamous marriages for the purposes of succession and legitimacy.

Having established that it was necessary to modify English law in its application to the local inhabitants to avoid injustice and oppression,[60] the next problem for the courts was deciding when modification was warranted on those grounds.

Judicial decisions over the years seem to indicate that, as with British colonial policy in India and Pakistan,[61] such modifications were made primarily in family law and related areas (*e.g.* marriage,

---

[56] *Id.*
[57] *Id.*, at p. 81.
[58] (1858) 3 Ky. 16 at 31-33.
[59] See *Cheang Thye Phin* v. *Tan Ah Loy* [1920] A.C. 369; *Khoo Hooi Leong* v. *Khoo Hean Kwee* [1926] A.C. 529; *Khoo Hooi Leong* v. *Khoo Chong Yeok* [1930] A.C. 346. However, the theoretical justification for applying personal law and the extent of its application, have never been adequately defined: see Bartholomew, *supra*, n. 42 at p. 92.
[60] *Khoo Hooi Leong* v. *Khoo Chong Yeok, supra*, n. 59.
[61] See David & Brierley, *supra*, n. 43 at pp. 491 and 495; Zweigert and Kotz, *supra*, n. 43 at p. 234; R.B. Schlesinger, *Comparative Law: Cases-Text-Materials* (4th ed. 1980), pp. 308-309.

divorce, adoption and succession)[62] *i.e.*, areas which least conflicted with British commercial interests. Thus, for example, Chinese polygamous marriages were recognised so that secondary wives and their children could be provided for under the Statute of Distributions.[63]

However, where modification entailed an impingement on British commercial interests, as in the case of devises in perpetuity that violated the principle of free alienability of land (which principle was vital to economic growth), then such modification was not easily forthcoming.[64] Hence, in fields of law such as contract, commercial law, procedure, evidence and other areas generally, English law of general application virtually displaced indigenous law completely.[65] Native law and customs were generally not tolerated in these areas. This was in line with the wider British colonial policy of ensuring the general uniformity of law throughout the British empire.[66]

Thus, personal law generally came to be accommodated only in family law matters. This remains the position in Singapore today. However, the scope of application of personal law has been greatly reduced since the enactment of the Women's Charter in 1961.[67] This legislation set up a common, unified law on marriage and divorce to govern all ethno-religious groups in Singapore except Muslims.[68] As a result, Chinese and Hindu customary law on marriage and divorce have been rendered largely irrelevant. However, there remain some

---

[62] See Braddell, *supra*, n. 14 at pp. 86-96; M.B. Hooker, *A Concise Legal History of South-East Asia* (1978), pp. 129-138.

[63] *Supra*, n. 59. It seems to this writer that a rigid adherence to the English concept of monogamous marriage here would have served no economic end, and would have worked injustice and oppression on those affected.

[64] See *Yeap Cheah Neo* v. *Ong Cheng Neo* (1875) L.R. 6 P.C. 381.

[65] This was generally the experience of British colonies elsewhere as well: see Schlesinger, *supra*, n. 61 at pp. 308-309. Thus, for example, the Statute of Frauds (29 Car. ii, c. 3) was considered applicable in the colony: see *Revely and Co.* v. *Kam Kong Gay and Anor.* (1840) 1 Ky. 32; so was the rule against perpetuities: see Braddell, *supra*, n. 14 at pp. 74-75; see also R. Braddell, *The Law of the Straits Settlements: A Commentary: Vol. 2* (2nd ed. 1932), pp. 28, 73, 165.

[66] See *e.g. Trimble* v. *Hill* (1879) App. Cas. 342 at 345, in which the Privy Council said: "[I]t is of the utmost importance that in all parts of the empire where English law prevails, the interpretation of that law by the Courts should be as nearly as possible the same".

[67] Cap. 47, Reprint 1981. Unless otherwise indicated, all "Cap." references hereinafter refer to the Singapore Statutes, Rev. Ed. 1970.

[68] See *infra*, Chapter I.D. Singapore Muslims are predominantly Malay although some 10% are of Indian and other non-Malay extraction. In 1980, Muslims made up 16% of the population: see *Singapore 1985*, p. 32.

situations in which Chinese customary law might still be relevant.[69] Generally, however, Muslim law[70] is the only personal law that continues to be of some significance in Singapore today.

3. The General Reception of English Law is Subject to Local Legislation.

Where there is local legislation governing a particular matter, English law is generally precluded from applying.[71] The body of local legislation has grown steadily since the nineteenth century.[72]

From 1833 to 1867, the Straits Settlements were a mere Residency under the administration of the governor in Bengal. The Charter Act of 1833 gave the Governor-General of India in Council power to legislate for all territories administered by the East India Company. This included the Straits Settlements. Thus, from 1833 to 1867, the main body of local legislation which qualified the general reception of English law was these "Indian Acts." In addition, the "Imperial Acts"[73] applicable to India also applied to the Straits Settlements.

In 1867, the Straits Settlements were made a separate Crown colony and transferred to the control of the Colonial Office in

---

[69] For example, if a couple who contracted a Chinese customary marriage prior to the commencement of the Women's Charter want a divorce, they would, *inter alia*, have to show the court that there was a valid marriage in the first place. Since the Women's Charter (s. 166) preserves the validity of customary marriages contracted prior to the commencement of the Charter, the validity of the couple's marriage would be determined by reference to Chinese customary law. Chinese customary law may also be relevant in determining the lawful wife (or wives) and children of a deceased man who married under Chinese custom before the commencement of the Women's Charter, for the purposes of succession to property. See Myint Soe, *The General Principles of Singapore Law* (Rev Reprint 1982), p. 28; Ahmad Ibrahim, *Family Law in Malaysia and Singapore* (2nd ed 1984), p. 38.

[70] Which is further modified by Malay custom where Malay Muslims are concerned: see *infra*, Chapter II.E.

[71] Braddell, *supra*, n. 14 at p. 72. See generally, Bartholomew, *supra*, n. 42 pp. 92 *et seq.*

[72] For a general discussion of the local legislation applicable in the Straits Settlements, see Bartholomew, *supra*, n. 42 at 92-97; see also, Braddell, *supra*, n. 14 at pp. 1-72.

[73] As a matter of statutory interpretation, statutes enacted by the English Parliament are generally regarded as being applicable only in England unless the statute provides otherwise, either expressly or by necessary implication. In such a case, the statute is known as an "Imperial Act", *i.e.*, applicable to Singapore because of the "imperial legislative authority of the English Parliament": see Bartholomew, *supra*, n. 41, p. xliv.

London.[74] Thereafter, the Indian Legislative Council ceased to legislate for the Straits Settlements. Its place was taken over by the new Legislative Council of the Straits Settlements. With that, the period of the Indian Acts ended and that of the Straits Settlements Acts and Ordinances began. In spite of this change in political and legal administration, legal continuity was ensured by virtue of the Government of the Straits Settlements Act,[75] which provided that the laws in existence in the Straits Settlements at the date of the transfer would continue in force.

Thus, after 1867, the law of England as it stood on 27 November 1826, subject to local circumstances and local legislation, continued in force in Singapore, as did pre-1867 Indian Acts that had applied to the Straits Settlements and pre-1867 Imperial Acts that had applied to India. Therefore, up to 1946 (when the Straits Settlements were disbanded), these latter two legislative sources, together with the Straits Settlements Acts and Ordinances and post-1867 Imperial Acts which applied to the Straits Settlements,[76] constituted the local legislation to which the general reception of English law under the Second Charter was subject.

Although the Straits Settlements were occupied by the Japanese from 1942 to 1945,[77] this period of Japanese rule left no lasting imprint on the legal system of the Straits Settlements for two major reasons. First, it was too brief a period for any of the legal changes introduced by the Japanese administration to take root. Secondly, all laws enacted by the Japanese during the occupation were repealed when the British regained control of the Straits Settlements after the war ended in 1945.[78]

In 1946, the Straits Settlements were disbanded. Singapore became a separate colony and continued as such till 1959, when internal

---

[74] By virtue of the Government of the Straits Settlements Act 1866, 29 & 30 Vic. c. 115.
[75] *Id.*, s. 4.
[76] For example, the Copyright Act 1911. This Act is still law in Singapore: see *Butterworths & Co. (Publishers) Ltd. & Ors.* v. *Ng Sui Nam* [1985]1 M.L.J. 196, H.C. For various reasons, it is not always easy to ascertain the applicability of any given Imperial Act: see Bartholomew, *supra,* n. 41. pp. xlviii-l.
[77] For a brief account of the state of legal affairs in Singapore during the Japanese Occupation, see Goh Kok Leong, "A Legal History of the Japanese Occupation in Singapore" [1981] 1 M.L.J. xx.
[78] S.K. Das, *Japanese Occupation and Ex Post Facto Legislation in Malaya* (1959), p. 28; Bartholomew, *supra,* n. 41, p. li.

Legal History 13

self-government was granted and the State of Singapore was created. In 1963, Singapore became a constituent state in the Federation of Malaysia. Two years later, in 1965, Singapore seceded from the Federation of Malaysia and has been an independent republic since then. During each of these successive phases of political and constitutional change dating from 1946, Singapore had its own legislative body. The legislative period from 1946 to 1962 has been described as the period of Singapore Acts and Ordinances.[79] Between 1963 and 1965, Malaysian federal legislation was also applicable in Singapore. Since 1965, the republic's parliament has also enacted a considerable amount of legislation.[80] Thus, since 1946, the body of local legislation to which the general reception of English law is subject, has been increasingly augmented, and will continue to expand in the future.

There is yet another aspect of general reception that requires mention. This is the distinction between the general reception of English statutes and English case-law. There is a cut-off date for the reception of English statutes, but apparently none for English case-law. As early as 1835, the colonial courts had already held that under the Second Charter, only pre-1826 English law was received.[81] The exclusion of post-1826 English statutes was based on a principle of statutory interpretation that English statutes apply only in England unless the statute expressly or by necessary implication provides otherwise.[82] Thus, post-1826 English statutes were not received in Singapore. However, the position was different with regard to English common law or case-law, which has long continued to be received even where it was of post-1826 vintage.[83] For example, the 1932 landmark English case of *Donoghue* v. *Stevenson*[84] which laid the foundation for the modern English law of negligence, has been readily applied in Singapore.[85] The reasons for the continuing reception of English case law in Singapore are discussed in Chapter II.D.

---

[79] G.W. Bartholomew, "Sources and Literature of Singapore Law" in Malaya Law Review Legal Essays (1975), p. 325.
[80] Contained in the Singapore Statutes, Rev. Ed. 1970, and the Annual Supplements thereto.
[81] Braddell, *supra*, n. 14 at p. 27. See *e.g. Municipal Commissions* v. *Tolson* (1872) 1 Ky. 272.
[82] See Bartholomew, *supra*, n. 42 at p. 90.
[83] *Id.*, at pp. 89-90.
[84] [1932] A.C. 562.
[85] See *K.M.A. Abdul Rahim & Anor.* v. *Owners of "Lexa Maersk" & Ors.* [1973] 2 M.L.J. 121 at 125-126, and *Dobb & Co. Ltd.* v. *Hecla* [1973] 2 M.L.J. 128 at 129-130, both High Court decisions; *infra*, Chapter II.D.

C. Specific Reception of English Law

Apart from the general reception of English Law under the Second Charter which imported English case-law and pre-1826 English statutes, English law has been subsequently received in specific areas through other means. The most significant example is the continuing reception of English law on mercantile matters.

1. Section 5 of the Civil Law Act

Although the colonial courts had established that under the Second Charter only pre-1826 English law was received, in practice, post-1826 English statutes continued to be applied in commercial matters because the local bench and bar were English-trained.[86] This practice was finally given statutory ukase in the Straits Settlements by section 6 of the Civil Law Ordinance 1878,[87] which directed the courts, whenever they entertained mercantile issues, to apply the current English law unless there was local legislation governing the matter. As pointed out by Professor Hickling, this provision was really an instance of legislation catching up with or confirming the practice of the courts.[88] It has survived several re-enactments of the Civil Law Ordinance and is section 5 of the Civil Law Act today.[89] This provision constitutes the backbone of Singapore mercantile law and covers a wide range of English statutes and common law.

Although more than a century has elapsed since the inception of section 5, the precise scope of commercial reception under it unfortunately remains uncertain.[90] The only two Privy Council decisions on this point[91] did little to elucidate matters because their Lordships

---

[86] Kyshe, "Judicial-Historical Preface" 1 Ky. i.
[87] Ord. No. 4 of 1878.
[88] R.H. Hickling, "Section 5 of the Civil Law Act: Snark or Boojum?" (1972) 21 Mal. L.R. 351 at 352.
[89] Cap. 30, as amended by Act No. 24 of 1979.
[90] See G.W. Bartholomew, "The Singapore Statute Book" (1984) 26 Mal. L.R. 1 at 13, 15; Chan Sek Keong, "The Civil Law Ordinance, Section 5(1): A Re-appraisal" [1961] M.L.J. lvii; R.H. Hickling, "Section 5 of the Civil Law Act: Snark or Boojum?" (1979) 21 Mal. L.R. 351; Soon Choo Hock and Andrew Phang Boon Leong, "Reception of English Commercial Law in Singapore — A Century of Uncertainty" in *The Common Law in Singapore and Malaysia* (A.J. Harding ed. 1985), pp. 33-74.
[91] *Seng Djit Hin* v. *Nagurdas Purshotumdas & Co.* [1928] A.C. 444; *Shaik Sahied bin Abdullah Bajerai* v. *Sockalingam Chettiar* [1933] A.C. 342.

rendered two somewhat irreconcilable judgments.[92] The combined effect of the desire to eradicate the uncertainties plaguing section 5, and the growing concern that British membership in the European Economic Community might develop English mercantile law in directions unsuited to Singapore, led the Singapore Parliament to amend section 5 in 1979.[93] The amendments were aimed at clarifying the scope of section 5 and putting some brakes on the "blanket" application of English law in mercantile issues. Thus, for example, according to the Explanatory Statement appended to the Bill and the Minister for Home Affairs when he presented the Bill before Parliament, the

---

[92] For a discussion of the two decisions, see Soon Choo Hock and Andrew Phang Boon Leong, *supra*, n. 90 at pp. 41-48; G.W. Bartholomew. "The Reception of English Law Overseas" (1968) 9 Me Judice 1. There are different views on the effect of the decisions and whether they are reconcilable. See *e.g.* D.K.K. Chong "Section 5 Thing-Um-A-Jig!" [1982] 1 M.L.J. c at ci.

[93] See Singapore Parliamentary Debates Official Report, Vol. 39, No. 7, 21 September 1979, cols. 445-446. As amended by the Civil Law (Amendment No. 2) Act, No. 24 of 1979, s. 5 now reads:

5.(1) *Subject to the provisions of this section*, in all questions or issues which arise or which have to be decided in Singapore with respect to the law of partnerships, corporations, banks and banking, principals and agents, carriers by air, land and sea, marine insurance, average, life and fire insurance, and with respect to mercantile law generally, the law *with respect to those matters* to be administered shall be the same as would be administered in England in the like case, at the corresponding period, if such question or issue had arisen or had to be decided in England, unless in any case other provision is or shall be made by any law having force in Singapore.

(2) Nothing *in this section* shall be taken to introduce into Singapore —

(a) any part of the law of England relating to the tenure or conveyance or assurance of, or succession to, any immovable property, or any estate, right or interest therein;

(b) any law enacted or made in the United Kingdom, whether before or after the commencement of the Civil Law (Amendment No. 2) Act, 1979 —

(i) giving effect to a treaty or international agreement to which Singapore is not a party; or

(ii) regulating the exercise of any business or activity by providing for registration, licensing or any other method of control or by the imposition of penalties; and

(c) any provision contained in any Act of Parliament of the United Kingdom where there is a written law in force in Singapore corresponding to that Act.

(3) *For the purposes of this section —*

(a) the law of England which is to be administered by virtue of subsection (1) shall be subject to such modifications and adaptations as the circumstances of Singapore may require; and

(b) a written law in force in Singapore shall be regarded as corresponding to an Act of Parliament of the United Kingdom under paragraph (c) of subsection (2) if (notwithstanding that it differs, whether to a small extent or substantially from that Act) the purpose or purposes of the written law are the same or similar to those of that Act.

[The words inserted by the 1979 amendment are italicised for ease of comparison.]

amendment was intended to confine the reception of English law under section 5 to English mercantile law only.[94] However, according to English authorities (which are likely to be followed in Singapore), parliamentary proceedings (*i.e.* Hansard) cannot be relied upon as an aid to statutory interpretation.[95] It also appears that explanatory memoranda attached to Bills may not be looked at for the purpose of ascertaining parliamentary intention.[96] If this is the position, and since statutory interpretation is necessarily subjective, it is still possible to read the amended provision as importing the whole of English law and not just English mercantile law.

Section 5 also excludes any U.K. law which is the direct result of treaties or international agreements to which Singapore is not a party.[97] In addition, it excludes any U.K. law regulating the exercise of any business or activity by providing for registration, licensing or any other method of control, or by the imposition of penalties.[98] Such legislation is logically excluded because they may create or presuppose machinery or procedures which do not exist, or are not possible to operate in Singapore. Section 5 further prohibits the reception of any provision in a U.K. Act if there is a Singapore Act which has the same or similar purpose(s) as that U.K. Act. This is so even though the two Acts may in fact be quite different in substance.[99] The problem here is the meaning to be assigned to the words "similar purpose." What degree of similarity of purpose is necessary to preclude a potentially applicable English statute? Finally, section 5 also expressly stipulates that the English law to be administered thereunder is to be "subject to such modifications and adaptations as the circumstances of Singapore may require."[100] The question here is this: under what circumstances will English law be modified? The

---

[94] See Singapore Government Gazette Bills Supplement, Bill No. 25/79, p. 3; Singapore Parliamentary Debates Official Report, Vol. 39, No. 7, 21 September 1979, col. 447.
[95] See *Black-Clawson International Ltd.* v. *Papierwerke Waldhof-Aschaffenburg A.G.* [1975] 1 All E.R. 810; *Davis* v. *Johnson* [1978] 1 All E.R. 1132.
[96] See *Raja Shariman & Che Tak* v. *C.A. Ribeiro & Co. Ltd.* (1921) 1 M.C. 57 at 62-63, Supreme Court of the Straits Settlements (Singapore).
[97] s. 5(2) (b) (i).
[98] s. 5(2) (b) (ii). This is a statutory endorsement of the Privy Council's *dicta* in *Shaik Sahied bin Abdullah Bajerai* v. *Sockalingam Chettiar, supra*, n. 91 at p. 346.
[99] ss. 5(2) (c) and 5(3) (b).
[100] s. 5(3) (a). This qualification was absent from the old provision, but was nevertheless read into it by the Privy Council without relying on any authority: see *Shaik Sahied bin Abdullah Bajerai* v. *Sockalingam Chettiar, supra*, n. 91 at p. 347.

amendment clearly gives judges discretion and flexibility to screen out English statutes unsuited to the circumstances of Singapore. However, it offers no guidelines or criteria for the exercise of this power. The 1979 amendment is therefore far from satisfactory. New grey areas which generate more uncertainty have been left in its wake, and these await judicial clarification. Thus, even after the 1979 amendment, it remains uncertain precisely which English statutes may be applicable in Singapore by virtue of section 5 of the Civil Law Act.

From the foregoing, it is clear why the law governing mercantile matters in Singapore continues to be closely linked with that of England. The problems attendant on preserving this *status quo* through the vehicle of section 5 are also quite apparent.

2. Other Provisions

Apart from commercial matters, English law continues to be received in other specific areas by way of "saving clauses" in Singapore statutes which permit references to English law in certain circumstances *e.g.* where there is a lacuna in the statute in question. Thus, section 101(2) of the Bills of Exchange Act[101] states:

> Subject to the provisions of any written law for the time being in force, the rules of the common law of England, including the law merchant, shall, save in so far as they are inconsistent with the express provisions of this Act, apply to bills of exchange, promissory notes and cheques.

Another example of this "legislation by reference"[102] is seen in section 5 of the Criminal Procedure Code[103] which provides:

> As regards matters of criminal procedure for which no special provision has been made by this Code or by any other law for the time being in force in Singapore the law relating to criminal procedure for the time being in force in England shall be applied so far as the same does not conflict or is not inconsistent with this Code and can be made auxiliary thereto.

---

[101] Cap. 28.
[102] See Bartholomew, *supra*, n. 42 at p. 95. Other examples of "legislation by reference" include s. 79 of the Women's Charter, Cap. 47; s. 62(1) of the Supreme Court of Judicature Act, Cap. 15; s. 201 of the Singapore Armed Forces Act 1972, No. 17 of 1972.
[103] Cap. 113, Reprint 1980.

"Legislation by reference" provisions inevitably raise the question of whether the reference is to current English law (*i.e.* continuing reception) or to English law as it stood at the date the provision was enacted (*i.e.* cut-off reception). This is essentially a question of construction depending on the wording and context of the provision involved.[104] Thus, for example, provisions such as section 5 of the Civil Law Act and section 5 of the Criminal Procedure Code by their express wording provide for a continuing reception of English law in the circumstances specified in each respective Act.

Decided cases involving section 5 of the Civil Law Act and other reception provisions are relatively few in number, and this may tempt some to surmise that in spite of the theoretical difficulties mentioned above, these provisions are perhaps not so problematic in practice and are therefore seldom litigated. Be that as it may, as was pointed out by Professor Bartholomew, such provisions are nevertheless unsatisfactory because they create legal uncertainty and "constitute hidden traps in that, depending upon how they are interpreted, they may attract the application of English statutes."[105] Since certainty in commercial law is especially important for economic growth and development, the ideal solution would be to authoritatively declare, once and for all, precisely which English statutes are applicable in Singapore, reproduce their text in the Singapore Statutes, and thereby do away with reception provisions.[106] In fact, another way in which English law has been transfused into the Singapore legal system has been through English statutes re-enacted *verbatim* in Singapore.[107] However, until the time such a step is taken, those who attempt to understand the Singapore legal system need to be aware of the potential relevance and applicability of English law in important areas of Singapore law such as mercantile matters. Although the Singapore Statutes contain the bulk of the legislation applicable in Singapore, they are not exhaustive.

In conclusion, it may be seen that the cumulative effect of the general reception of English law (under the 1826 Second Charter of Justice), specific reception by virtue of provisions such as section 5 of

---

[104] See *The Yuri* [1927] A.C. 915.
[105] Bartholomew, *supra*, n. 90 at p. 15.
[106] *Id.*
[107] See Bartholomew, *supra*, n. 42 at p. 96. Examples include the Bills of Exchange Act, Cap. 28; the Carriage of Goods By Sea Act, No. 30 of 1972; the Frustrated Contracts Act, Cap. 33.

the Civil Law Act and saving clauses in other local legislation, and English statutes or statutory provisions re-enacted *verbatim* in Singapore, was to firmly anchor the Singapore legal system in the English common law family. This remains the bedrock of the Singapore legal system today in spite of sweeping constitutional and political changes since the disbandment of the Straits Settlements in 1946.[108] Substantial legal continuity has been made possible by a series of provisions which ensured that the laws in operation at the date of such changes would continue in force.[109]

D. Other Legal Influences

Our picture of the foundations of the Singapore legal system would be incomplete without mentioning that although the Singapore legal system has borrowed heavily from English law, it has, to a lesser extent, also imbibed legal influences from other sources. For example, the Singapore Penal Code[110] and Criminal Procedure Code[111] were borrowed mainly from India in the nineteenth century.[112] More recently, Singapore borrowed the Torrens system of land registration from Australia. Singapore company law is also closer to the Australian than the English model. This phenomenon of borrowing from multiple legal sources is by no means a unique one because, to varying degrees, every legal system contains features or ideas borrowed from others at different points in time.[113]

At a much more fundamental level, exposure to successive layers of disparate legal influences can produce pluralism within a legal order. This means that, to some extent, different laws apply to different groups of people within a single country.[114] Legal pluralism

---

[108] See Bartholomew, *supra*, n. 42 at p. 97.
[109] See Bartholomew, *supra*, n. 41 at pp. l-lviii.
[110] Cap. 103. The Indian Penal Code was based primarily on English criminal law, which was itself mostly uncodified. However, the Code also considered some European models of criminal law, in particular, the French Penal Code: see Zweigert and Kotz, *supra*, n. 43 at p. 235.
[111] Cap. 113, Reprint 1980.
[112] See R. Braddell, *The Law of the Straits Settlements: A Commentary: Vol. 2* (2nd ed. 1932), pp. 73-74, 85-86.
[113] See M.B. Hooker, *Legal Pluralism: An Introduction to Colonial and Neo-Colonial Laws* (1975), pp. 1-5; Schlesinger, *supra*, n. 61 at p. 306; Levy, "The Reception of Highly Developed Legal Systems by Peoples of Different Cultures" (1950) 25 Wash. L.R. 233.
[114] See Schlesinger, *supra*, n. 61 at p. 326.

was the policy of many colonial powers[115] and is a surviving heritage in many former European colonies such as India, Indonesia, Malaysia and Singapore. In the case of Singapore, British colonisation superimposed English common law on the pre-existing Malay customary law and Muslim law.[116] The result is that, today, whilst the Singapore legal system is predominantly common law, there is a small degree of legal pluralism in that a separate system of Muslim law still governs the Muslim community in religious, matrimonial and related matters.[117] As previously explained,[118] this is the only area in the Singapore legal system where personal law continues to have some significance today. This personal law of the Muslim community is administered by a separate system of courts and judicial officers in accordance with the Administration of Muslim Law Act.[119]

However, in all other areas apart from family law and related matters, the Singapore legal system is a unitary one in that there is a single body of law which is universally applicable to all sections of the population. And, as previously explained, the bedrock of this unitary body of law is the English common law bestowed by colonial heritage.

---

[115] *Id.* See generally, Hooker, *Legal Pluralism: An Introduction to Colonial and Neo-Colonial Laws* (1975).
[116] When the British first arrived in Singapore in 1819, the island had already been inhabited by Malay people for at least five centuries: see *Singapore 1985*, p. 45. Islam had reached the Malay peninsula in the fourteenth century and had spread quickly throughout it with the territorial expansion of the Malacca Sultanate in the fifteenth century: see K.G. Tregonning, *A History of Modern Malaysia and Singapore* (Rev. 2nd ed. 1972), pp. 16-21. When the British arrived in 1819, Singapore was under the rule of the Sultan of Johore. The island was inhabited by the Temenggong (a "defence minister" of the Sultan) and a handful of fishermen. The Temenggong exercised a jurisdiction over the fishermen in accordance with Malay law and custom: see Braddell, *supra*, n. 14 at pp. 22-23.
[117] This is also true of the legal system of Malaysia: see Hashim Yeop A. Sani, *Our Constitution* (1980), pp. 149-158; Ahmad Ibrahim, *The Malaysian Legal System* (1970), pp. 475-570.
[118] *Supra*, Chapter I.B.2.
[119] Cap. 42.

Chapter II

Sources of Law

Against a background understanding of the historical foundations of the Singapore legal system, we can proceed to consider more specific aspects of it, beginning with the sources of Singapore law. This topic examines the nature of the legal rules that make up Singapore law *i.e.*, the legal rules which Singapore courts apply in order to determine disputes.

The rules that make up Singapore law emanate from a variety of sources which carry differing degrees of legal authority. Sources of law may be generally classified as written or unwritten law. In the event of conflict, written law generally prevails over unwritten law. The former refers to "enacted law" *i.e.* any law enacted by a body possessing legislative powers. In descending order of legal authority, Singapore's written law[1] comprises the Constitution, legislation and subsidiary legislation. Conversely, unwritten law refers to "unenacted law." The primary source of unwritten law is judicial precedents or case-law. Custom constitutes a relatively minor source of unwritten law. Each of these sources of law will now be discussed in greater detail.

A. The Constitution

The Constitution lies at the apex of the hierarchy of Singapore law. It lays down the fundamental principles and basic framework of state organisation as well as enshrines the fundamental rights of the individual *vis-a-vis* the state.[2] The Constitution is the supreme law of the land. This means that any Act of Parliament which is inconsistent with the Constitution will be void to the extent of such inconsistency.[3]

---

[1] For a detailed account of the written laws of Singapore, see G.W. Bartholomew, "Introduction" in *Tables of the Written Laws of the Republic of Singapore: 1819-1971, Vol. 1 — Local Legislation* (compiled by E. Srinivasagam and staff of the Law Library, University of Singapore, 1972), (hereinafter "Introduction"); "Sources and Literature of Singapore Law" (1982) 2 Lawasia N.S. 1.

[2] *E.g.*, equality, freedom of religion, *etc.*: see Part IV, Reprint of the Constitution of the Republic of Singapore 1980.

[3] Art. 4. Unless otherwise indicated, all references to "Art/(s)." in this work are to the Reprint of the Constitution of the Republic of Singapore 1980, as amended by Acts No. 24 of 1980, No. 7 of 1981, No. 16 of 1984 and No. 10 of 1985.

In this respect, the Singapore legal system is markedly different from its English counterpart in that although Singapore borrowed the parliamentary system of government from England, the Singapore system is premised on a written constitution and constitutional supremacy whereas that of the U.K. is founded on an unwritten constitution and parliamentary sovereignty. What this means in theory is that the law-making powers of the Singapore Parliament are limited (by the Constitution) whereas those of the U.K. Parliament are theoretically unlimited. The practical ramification of this is that Singapore judges have the power to strike down both legislative and executive acts for unconstitutionality whereas English judges can only strike down executive acts (but not legislative acts since the English Parliament is supreme).[4] In practice, however, Singapore judges have rarely exercised this power.[5]

It should however be pointed out that, apart from one important exception mentioned below, the Constitution is relatively easy to amend. Constitutional amendment can be performed by a law enacted by the legislature, provided that at the Bill stage, such law received the support of two-thirds of the total parliamentary membership on both the second and third readings.[6] In current Singapore practice, statutes often receive this kind of support in the process of enactment,[7] and the problem that this creates is whether a statute which complies with the constitutional amendment procedure outlined above but does not expressly state that it is a constitutional amendment, is to be struck down as unconstitutional or upheld as an implied amendment to the Constitution.[8] However, few problems have sprung from this in practice because the constitutionality of legislation is rarely challenged in the courts.

---

[4] However, this does not mean that English judges are completely powerless to counter (what they may consider to be) legislative excesses. Their constitutional role in interpreting statutes allows them to exercise a certain amount of legislative power and temper the effect of legislation. Cases interpreting legislation become as much a source of law as the legislation interpreted.

[5] This is partly because constitutional issues are seldom litigated. This phenomenon is possibly linked to the legal culture of Singapore: see *infra*, Chapter VI.A.

[6] Art. 5.

[7] This is because the Singapore Parliament is heavily dominated by the ruling People's Action Party. This has been the position for the last twenty years or so: see *Singapore 1985*, pp. 270-271. The present Parliament has 2 opposition Members of Parliament compared to 77 belonging to the ruling party.

[8] It has been suggested that the only way to reconcile arts. 4 and 5 is to exclude implied amendments: see Bartholomew, "Introduction", *supra*, n. 1 at p. xlviii.

A much more stringent procedure is required for any attempt to amend Part III of the Constitution which relates to protection of the sovereignty of Singapore. An attempt to amend this part of the Constitution must first be preceded by a two-third majority of the total number of registered voters[9] at a national referendum.

B. Statutes

Statutes (or legislation) are next in the hierarchy of laws in Singapore. They are laws enacted by the Singapore Parliament. This would also include the laws enacted by bodies (such as the Governor-General of India in Council and the Legislative Council of the Straits Settlements) which had power to legislate for Singapore in previous times. Such legislation may still be in force today if it has not yet been repealed. Thus, legislation in force in Singapore today may emanate from different periods of legislative history, which are briefly outlined as follows[10]:

(1) 1834-1867: Indian Acts, and pre-1867 Imperial Acts applicable to India;
(2) 1867-1942: Straits Settlements Acts and Ordinances;
(3) 1942-1945: Japanese legislation; however, all such legislation was repealed after the war when the British returned[11];
(4) 1946-1963: Singapore Acts and Ordinances, and Imperial Acts enacted between 1867 and 1963;
(5) 1963-1965: Malaysian federal legislation,[12] and Singapore State legislation;
(6) 1965 to date: Republic of Singapore Acts.

However, as previously explained,[13] it is important to note that even the sum total of the above legislation would still be an incomplete statement of the statutory law in force in Singapore. This is because, apart from the general reception of English law under the Second Charter, English law (both statutes and case-law) continues to filter in by virtue of "legislation by reference" devices such as section 5 of the Civil Law Act and other specific reception provisions or "saving" clauses.

---

[9] Arts. 6-8.
[10] See *supra*, Chapter I.A.3. For a more detailed account of Singapore's legislative history, see Bartholomew, "Introduction" *supra*, n. 1 at pp. xvi-l.
[11] See Bartholomew, "Introduction", *supra*, n. 1 at p. li.
[12] *Id.*, at pp. lxxi-lxxiii.
[13] See *supra*, Chapter I.C.2.

Since Singapore joined the common law family in the nineteenth century, legislation has become an increasingly important source of law. This has been particularly the case in the twentieth century, and is a development shared by many other countries. In many common law countries, legislation continues to encroach upon the common law and outgrow it in importance for a number of reasons. First, legislation enables a comprehensive and systematic treatment of a particular topic or area of the law. Secondly, it is sometimes necessary to use legislation to change or update outmoded common law rules. Thirdly, legislation has stepped in to regulate whole new areas (such as environmental law) which had hitherto never been dealt with by the common law. Fourthly, for many countries, legislation is an increasingly important instrument for implementing government policy and social engineering. Thus, legislation will continue to grow in importance. The only constraint on Singapore legislation is that it must not be inconsistent with the Constitution.[14] Legislation will also be increasingly likely to encroach on areas traditionally governed by the common law (such as tort and contract). Thus, it may be seen that although most of the rules that make up English contract law are still to be found in the cases, statutes such as the Misrepresentation Act 1967[15] and the Unfair Contract Terms Act 1977[16] have been making inroads into the common law.[17]

Nevertheless, the judiciary continues to play an important role because it is charged with the important responsibility of interpreting and applying legislation. In doing so, its primary duty is to ascertain the intention of parliament as expressed in the statute, and, provided the statute is constitutional, to give effect to it. Although judges do, in fact, make law interstitially in the process of interpreting a statute, it is still generally not acceptable for them to fill gaps in the law (*i.e.*, to make law too blatantly). Doing so might be viewed as encroaching on the legislative function which is still widely regarded as one that properly belongs to parliament.

---

[14] This, however, begs the question whether the Constitution may be impliedly amended by an inconsistent statute: see *infra*, Chapter III.A.
[15] c. 7.
[16] c. 50.
[17] These English Acts are probably applicable in Singapore by virtue of s. 5 of the Civil Law Act, Cap. 30. See Soon Choo Hock and Andrew Phang Boon Leong, "Reception of English Commercial Law in Singapore — A Century of Uncertainty" in *The Common Law in Singapore and Malaysia* (A.J. Harding, ed. 1985) at p.74.

Sources of Law 25

What principles do Singapore judges follow in interpreting statutes? Very few Singapore cases actually discuss the principles of statutory interpretation in Singapore. Nevertheless, it seems clear that English principles of statutory interpretation are generally adhered to.

In ascertaining parliamentary intention in a statute, the judiciary has the assistance of a variety of aids which may be generally categorised as intrinsic and extrinsic aids. Intrinsic aids are those found within the statute itself. They focus on the language used in the statute. Thus, intrinsic aids include the preamble, the long title, marginal notes, headings, punctuation and interpretation sections within the Act itself. In addition, English judges have developed a variety of competing approaches such as the "literal" rule,[18] the "golden" rule,[19] the "mischief" rule,[20] and the "purposive" approach,[21] all of which are avowedly aimed at ascertaining the parliamentary intention in a statute. Well-known common law canons or maxims of statutory interpretation such as *noscitur a sociis*,[22] *ejusdem generis*[23] and *expressio unius est exclusio alterius*[24] were also developed by judges. So, too, was the established principle of interpretation that penal or revenue statutes are to be strictly construed (*i.e.*, where there is an ambiguity, they should be interpreted in favour of the individual). However, it must be pointed out at this juncture that all these so-called "rules of interpretation" are not really rules at all. This is because there is no certainty that a given

---

[18] This rule advocates giving the words construed their literal meaning regardless of whether the result is sensible or not": M. Zander, *The Law-Making Process* (2nd ed. 1985), p.75.

[19] This rule directs the court to follow the literal approach unless it leads to absurdity or inconvenience or inconsistency, in which case the court should search for some other meaning: *id.*, at p. 77. For a modern formulation of the "golden" rule, see *Maunsell* v. *Olins* [1975] 1 All E.R. 16 at 25-26, and *Farrell* v. *Alexander* [1976] 2 All E.R. 721 at 734-735, per Lord Simon in both cases.

[20] This rule is also known as the rule in *Heydon's Case* (1584) 3 Co. Rep. 73. This approach requires the court to consider the common law before the Act, the mischief and defect for which the common law did not provide, the remedy appointed by parliament and the true reason for it: Zander, *supra*, n. 18 at p. 77.

[21] This approach focuses on the legislative purpose behind a statute rather than its literal meaning: see *e.g.*, Lord Diplock in *Kammins Ballrooms Co. Ltd.* v. *Zenith Investments (Torquay) Ltd.* [1971] A.C. 850 at 879-880.

[22] *I.e.*, the meaning of a word can be gathered from the context.

[23] *I.e.*, where general words follow specific words, the meaning of the general words will be confined to the class indicated by the specific words.

[24] *I.e.*, that which is expressly mentioned excludes that which is not.

"rule" of interpretation will always be applied in every situation in which it is potentially applicable. Many situations in fact attract the application of competing "rules" and it is difficult to predict which will be given precedence over the others.

By contrast, extrinsic aids are those found outside the statute itself. Thus, the Interpretation Act,[25] for example, defines a number of terms and contains other provisions which are useful in interpreting statutes and subsidiary legislation. Other extrinsic aids include those which throw light on the legislative history of the statute *e.g.* the official committee reports leading to the enactment of the statute, explanatory statements appended to the draft Bill, and the printed reports of parliamentary debates.[26] However, like their English counterparts, Singapore judges are generally rather conservative, and therefore, apart from the Interpretation Act, they usually confine themselves to intrinsic aids when they interpret a statute. Even so, there is a considerable array of intrinsic aids available and no general rules as to their relative importance. Thus, in the final analysis, statutory interpretation remains an essentially subjective process which "ultimately turns on impalpable and indefinable elements of judicial spirit or attitude."[27]

C. Subsidiary Legislation[28]

As in many other countries, it has become an increasingly common practice in Singapore for statutes to confer powers on ministers or other persons or bodies to make rules or regulations for specified purposes. These rules or regulations are referred to as subsidiary, delegated or subordinate legislation. The Interpretation Act defines "subsidiary legislation" to mean:

> any order in council, proclamation, rule, regulation, order, notification, by-law or other instrument made under any Act, Ordinance or other lawful authority and having legislative effect.[29]

Under this definition, important instruments such as the Second Charter of Justice 1826 and the Singapore (Constitution) Order in

---

[25] Cap. 3.
[26] Known in England as "Hansard."
[27] C. K. Allen, *Law in the Making* (7th ed. 1978), p. 529.
[28] See also Myint Soe, *The General Principles of Singapore Law* (Rev. Reprint 1982). pp. 51-54. For a detailed treatment of this topic, see M.P. Jain, *Administrative Law of Malaysia and Singapore* (1980), pp. 31-126.
[29] Cap. 3, s. 2.

Council 1958[30] are not statutes but subsidiary legislation. Thus, it can be seen that subsidiary legislation can have as significant and far-reaching an impact as statutes.

The main justification for the growing use of subsidiary legislation lies in the fact that modern legislatures work under severe time and other constraints which make it more efficient to have statutes laying down the outline and general principles, leaving the details to be subsequently filled in by the relevant ministers or administrative authorities. Such an arrangement is particularly necessary in the case of statutes such as the Road Traffic Act[31] which deal with technical matters and require many detailed regulations. Subsidiary legislation can also be brought into existence much more expeditiously than legislation. In addition, it is flexible because it can be amended as required from time to time without having to go through the cumbersome parliamentary process. Thus, subsidiary legislation saves parliamentary time and is both convenient and expedient.

On the other hand, subsidiary legislation is actually legislation by the executive. Therefore, it is viewed by some as a usurpation of legislative power by the executive. Since subsidiary legislation can have far-reaching effects on the lives of the people, and executive power to make such legislation may be open to abuse, it is only prudent that the power to make subsidiary legislation should be carefully controlled. Accordingly, subsidiary legislation is required to be constitutional and *intra vires*.[32]

Since the authoritative interpretation of subsidiary legislation is ultimately the task of the courts, the judiciary has a crucial role to play in preventing the abuse of executive power in making subsidiary legislation. In fact, judicial control of executive action provides much of the substance of administrative law. Administrative law is an important and relatively new field of judge-made law which has as its major aim, the protection of the citizen against abuse of power by the government.[33]

---

[30] [1958] 2 U.K. S.I., 2156 (No. 1956).
[31] Cap. 92, reprinted in 1973 incorporating amendments up to 1 May 1973 (see Reprint No. 1 of 1973).
[32] See *infra*, Chapter III.B.2.
[33] H.W.R. Wade, *Administrative Law* (5th ed. 1982), p. 5.

D. Judicial Precedents[34]

One distinctive feature of the common law tradition is the doctrine of *stare decisis, i.e.,* the doctrine of binding precedent. This doctrine compels inferior courts to follow the decisions of superior courts, and also directs certain courts to follow their own previous decisions. Thus, *stare decisis* may be said to operate both vertically and horizontally. The rationale behind the doctrine of binding precedent is as follows. First, justice requires similar treatment of similar cases. Secondly, the doctrine fosters legal certainty and orderly legal development.

However, not all parts of a decision have binding force. Only the *ratio decidendi* of the decision has this effect. The *ratio decidendi* is the rule of law on which the decision turns. It comprises the material facts and the decision thereon. Thus, remarks by judges on points of law not directly relevant to the issue in dispute have no binding force but are merely persuasive and are referred to as *obiter dicta*. Nevertheless, *dicta* can sometimes prove to be very persuasive in later cases, particularly if made by prominent judges.

From the foregoing, it will be seen that in order to apply the doctrine of *stare decisis*, one must first be able to extract the *ratio decidendi* of a previous decision since, theoretically, only that part has binding force. However, for several reasons, this is often not an easy task. For example, in cases with multiple judgments and as many different lines of reasoning, it is often difficult to ascertain the common denominator in the majority decision. In addition, there may be several abstractions of the *ratio* ranging from the specific to the general. The *ratio* is therefore often said to be a "fuzzy" concept. However, it is this very fuzziness which builds an important flexibility into the law and enables judges to develop the law to meet changing societal needs.[35]

Another prerequisite for the proper functioning of the doctrine of *stare decisis* is the existence of a comprehensive and efficient system

---

[34] For a general overview, see Myint Soe, *supra,* n. 28 at pp. 30-48.
[35] For more information on the application and development of case law, see J.H. Farrar and A.M. Dugdale, *Introduction to Legal Method* (2nd ed. 1984), pp. 81-121; W. Twining and D. Miers, *How to Do Things With Rules* (2nd ed. 1982), pp. 266-291.

Sources of Law 29

of law reporting. A heavy reliance on previous decisions as a source of law would not be possible otherwise. Law reporting in Singapore dates from the nineteenth century.[36] At present, however, there is no official law report for Singapore. The major law reporter is a private series of law reports called the *Malayan Law Journal* which began in 1932 and is published monthly.

Another presupposition of the doctrine of *stare decisis* is that it only applies to courts belonging to the same judicial hierarchy. Thus, it is necessary to know which courts belong to Singapore's judicial hierarchy. This requirement poses special problems for Singapore because her complicated political history makes it difficult to determine the predecessor courts of the present Singapore superior courts.

Although the doctrine of *stare decisis* was originally imported from England, it is important to note that the doctrine does not operate in exactly the same way in Singapore. However, a detailed discussion of the operation of *stare decisis* in Singapore and its attendant problems is beyond the scope of this work.[37] For present purposes, the reader must be content with a general outline.

Where vertical *stare decisis* is concerned, the position is relatively straightforward. The general rule is that the decisions of the higher courts are always binding on the lower courts. There are no exceptions to this rule. This is also the general English position. Thus, all decisions of the Privy Council on appeal from Singapore are binding on all Singapore courts.[38] Further, Privy Council appeals from other

---

[36] For a more detailed historical survey of law reporting in Singapore, see B.A. Mallal,"Law and Law Reporting in Malaya" (1959) 1 Mal. L.R. 71; G.W. Bartholomew, "Sources and Literature of Singapore Law" in *Malaya Law Review Legal Essays* (1975), pp. 314-324; "Sources and Literature of Singapore Law" (1982) 2 Lawasia N.S. 1 at 39-46.

[37] For a more detailed discussion of the operation of *stare decisis* in Singapore and Malaysia, see W. Woon, "Stare Decisis and Judicial Precedent in Singapore" in *The Common Law in Singapore and Malaysia* (A.J. Harding ed. 1985), pp. 115-139; "Precedents That Bind — A Gordian Knot: *Stare Decisis* in the Federal Court of Malaysia and the Court of Appeal, Singapore" (1982) 24 Mal. L.R. 1. See also Harbajan Singh, "*Stare Decisis* in Singapore and Malaysia — A Review" [1971] 1 M.L.J. xvi; M. Friedman, "Unscrambling the Judicial Egg: Some Observations on *Stare Decisis* in Singapore and Malaysia" (1980) 22 Mal. L.R. 227; Myint Soe, *supra*, n. 28 at pp. 43-47.

[38] See *Mah Kah Yew* v. *P.P.* [1971] 1 M.L.J. 1 at 3. Note, however, that this was a High Court pronouncement.

jurisdictions are binding on Singapore courts if they involve a statutory provision "which is word for word the same as the corresponding section of a local (*i.e.* Singapore) statute."[39] Similarly, the decisions of the Court of Appeal and the Court of Criminal Appeal are binding on the High Court and the subordinate courts. In turn, High Court decisions bind the subordinate courts.

In contrast, horizontal *stare decisis* is less consistent, and tends to diverge more from English practice. Beginning with the Privy Council, it may be noted that unlike the House of Lords, which bound itself till 1966,[40] the Privy Council has never regarded itself as being bound by its own previous decisions.[41]

Where the Court of Appeal is concerned, Singapore follows the English position as embodied in *Young* v. *Bristol Aeroplane Co. Ltd.*[42] Thus, the Court of Appeal is bound by its own previous decision unless:

(a) the previous decision cannot stand with a Privy Council decision; or

(b) there are two conflicting decisions of the Court of Appeal[43]; or

(c) the previous decision was given *"per incuriam."*[44]

Singapore's endorsement of the rule in *Young* v. *Bristol Aeroplane* was judicially confirmed by the Federal Court sitting in Singapore in 1964[45] and by the Singapore High Court in 1970.[46]

---

[39] See *Khalid Panjang* v. *P.P.* [1964] M.L.J. 108 at 111. This was a pronouncement by the Federal Court at a time when Singapore was part of Malaysia.
[40] See Practice Statement of 1966 [1966] 3 All E.R. 77. See also *Jones* v. *Secretary of State* [1972] 1 All E.R. 145.
[41] See *e.g. A.G. of St. Christopher, Nevis and Anguilla* v. *Reynolds* [1979] 3 All E.R. 129, per Lord Salmon.
[42] [1944] K.B. 718.
[43] In which case, the Court of Appeal has a choice.
[44] *I.e.,* in ignorance of an applicable judicial or statutory authority which would have affected the decision in the case.
[45] *Re Lee Gee Chong* [1965] M.L.J. 102 at 110, per Wee Chong Jin C.J. (Singapore).
[46] *Mah Kah Yew, supra,* n. 38, per Wee Chong Jin C.J. at 2-3. This was a somewhat curious situation in that the *High Court* appeared to be spelling out the rules of *stare decisis* in the Court of Appeal. However, this phenomenon is readily understood when one realises that the same judge sat in both *Re Lee Gee Chong* and *Mah Kah Yew.*

Sources of Law 31

However, the rule in *Young v. Bristol Aeroplane* does not apply to the Court of Criminal Appeal. Although the Court of Criminal Appeal will usually follow its own previous decisions, it has flexibility to depart from them in cases where the liberty of the individual is at stake.[47] This also follows the position in England.[48]

As regards the High Court, there are apparently no cases which have expressly determined whether the High Court binds itself.[49] Nevertheless, High Court practice appears to suggest that the High Court does not regard itself as being bound by its own previous decisions.[50]

Both the vertical and horizontal *stare decisis* outlined above may encounter problems when operating in the Singapore context primarily because the predecessor courts of the present Singapore Court of Appeal have yet to be authoritatively determined. It is necessary to identify these courts because their decisions have the same precedential effect as the decisions of the present Court of Appeal. This means that their decisions would bind the the Court of Appeal as well as lower courts such as the High Court and the subordinate courts. There is difficulty in identifying the Court of Appeal's proper predecessors because, since British colonisation of the Malay peninsula in the eighteenth century, the territory has undergone much political reorganisation which often entailed reorganisation of the court system as well. The situation will be better understood with the assistance of the diagram below.

From the diagram, it may be seen that the immediate predecessor of the present Singapore Court of Appeal is the Malaysian Federal Court.[51] This is because between 1963 and 1965, Singapore was part of Malaysia, and from 1965 to 1969, pending the establishment of the Singapore Court of Appeal, the Federal Court continued to hear appeals from Singapore. Thus, decisions of the Federal Court between 1963 and 1965, and Federal Court appeals from Singapore

---

[47] See *Mah Kah Yew, supra*, n. 38 at 3.
[48] *Rex v. Taylor* [1950] 2 K.B. 368.
[49] See W. Woon, "Precedents That Bind — A Gordian Knot: *Stare Decisis* in the Federal Court of Malaysia and the Court of Appeal, Singapore" (1982) 24 Mal. L.R. 1 at 14.
[50] *Id.*
[51] Which has been renamed the Mahkamah Agung, *i.e.* the Supreme Court, with effect from 1 January 1985: see [1985] 1 M.L.J. vii.

The Historical Evolution of the Singapore Court of Appeal

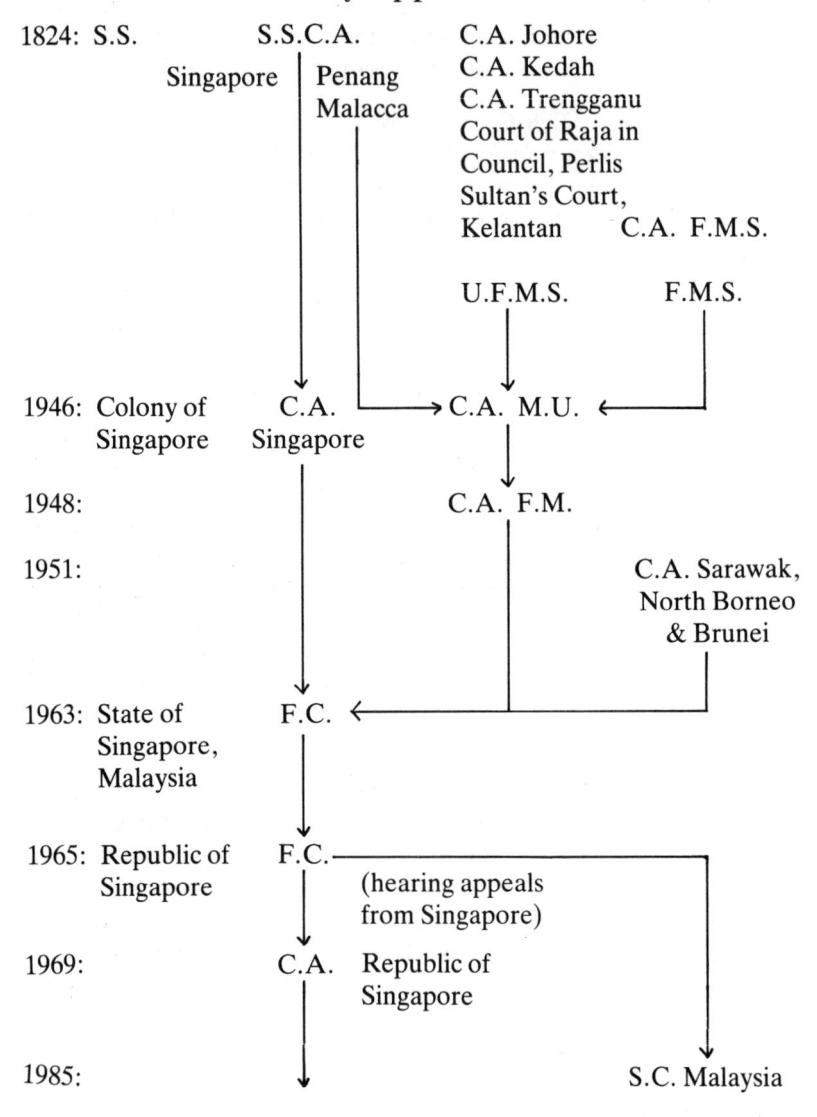

```
1824: S.S.              S.S.C.A.         C.A. Johore
            Singapore | Penang           C.A. Kedah
                      | Malacca          C.A. Trengganu
                                         Court of Raja in
                                         Council, Perlis
                                         Sultan's Court,
                                         Kelantan      C.A. F.M.S.

                                    U.F.M.S.           F.M.S.
                                       │                 │
                                       ▼                 │
1946: Colony of          C.A. ──────▶ C.A. M.U. ◀────────┘
      Singapore       Singapore
                                       │
                                       ▼
1948:                              C.A. F.M.

1951:                                              C.A. Sarawak,
                                                   North Borneo
                                                   & Brunei
                         │
                         ▼
1963: State of           F.C. ◀──────────────────────────┤
      Singapore,          │
      Malaysia            │

1965: Republic of        F.C. ───────────────────────────┤
      Singapore           │  (hearing appeals
                          │   from Singapore)
                          ▼
1969:                    C.A.  Republic of
                               Singapore
                          │                              │
                          ▼                              ▼
1985:                                              S.C. Malaysia
```

Legend: S.S. = Straits Settlements; C.A. = Court of Appeal; F.M.S. = Federated Malay States; U.F.M.S. = Unfederated Malay States; M.U. = Malayan Union; F.M. = Federation of Malaya; F.C. = Federal Court; S.C. = Supreme Court.

between 1965 and 1969[52] are clearly binding on the Singapore Court of Appeal today.[53] Working back one step further, decisions binding on the Federal Court between 1963 and 1965 would also be binding on the present Singapore Court of Appeal. What decisions then did the Federal Court between 1963 and 1965 regard as binding?

In *Re Lee Gee Chong*,[54] the Federal Court sitting in Singapore in 1964 held itself bound by a 1952 decision of the Court of Appeal of Singapore on the ground that, by virtue of section 88(3) of the Malaysia Act,[55] the Federal Court was to be regarded as being one and the same court as that former Singapore Court of Appeal.[56] This view was later reinforced in the Singapore High Court decision of *Mah Kah Yew* v. *P.P.*[57] by Wee Chong Jin C.J., who had also sat in the *Lee Gee Chong* case. In *Mah Kah Yew*, the High Court interpreted section 88(3) of the Malaysia Act to mean that only the Court of Appeal (Federation of Malaya), the Court of Appeal (Sarawak, North Borneo and Brunei) and the Court of Appeal/Court of Criminal Appeal (Singapore) were the proper predecessors of the Federal Court because they were expressly mentioned therein.[58] Thus, only these courts bound the Federal Court, and others, such as the Court of Appeal (F.M.S.), which were not expressly mentioned in section 88(3), did not bind the Federal Court. However, this position is somewhat difficult to reconcile with the case of *China Insurance* v. *Loong Moh*,[59] in which the Federal Court sitting in Singapore in 1964 held itself bound by a decision of the Straits Settlements Court of Appeal. This court preceded the Court of Appeal (Singapore) but was not expressly mentioned in section 88(3).

Thus, although there are cases which say that the decisions of the Straits Settlements Court of Appeal, the Court of Appeal (Singapore), the Court of Appeal (Federation of Malaya) and the Court of Appeal (Sarawak, North Borneo and Brunei) are binding on the

---

[52] See *Mah Kah Yew, supra*, n. 38 at 3.
[53] However, it remains an open question whether decisions of the Federal Court between 1965-69 on appeal from Malaysian states should similarly be binding on the Singapore Court of Appeal. The better view, however, is that they should not, since the Federal Court sitting in that capacity was arguably not part of the Singapore judicial hierarchy: see Woon, *supra*, n. 49 at p. 19; Myint Soe, *supra*, n. 28 at p. 44.
[54] [1965] 1 M.L.J. 102.
[55] No. 26 of 1963.
[56] *Supra*, n. 54 at p. 110, per Wee Chong Jin C.J.; p. 115, per Tan Ah Tah F.J.
[57] *Supra*, n. 38.
[58] For a criticism of this interpretation, see Woon, *supra*, n. 49 at pp. 15-17.
[59] [1964] M.L.J. 307.

present Singapore Court of Appeal, and that decisions of the Court of Appeal (F.M.S.) are not, some of these cases are not easy to reconcile. Also, it remains unclear whether decisions of the Malayan Union Court of Appeal bind the present Singapore Court of Appeal. These problems await judicial clarification.

Although it has been acknowledged that only local decisions (*i.e.* decisions of courts within the Singapore judicial hierarchy as previously outlined) bind Singapore courts,[60] English cases continue to exert a great deal of influence because of our colonial heritage. Singapore lawyers have long been strongly attached to English law because of their legal education and training, and the relative paucity of local legal literature and case-law. The nature of the influence of English case-law requires further examination.[61] In this regard, there are two types of English cases: those based on the common law, and those interpreting and applying English statutes which have been substantially adopted in Singapore. These two types of cases will be dealt with separately.

English decisions in common law areas such as tort and contract have always been highly influential in Singapore. What is the legal basis for this phenomenon? Do Singapore courts apply English common law decisions because of their persuasiveness or because they have the status of received law under the Second Charter? In the writer's opinion, the answer does not seem very clear. This is because the practice of applying English common law decisions in Singapore has been established for so long that Singapore courts seldom explain the basis on which they do so.[62] Thus, for example, common law doctrines embodied in English cases such as *Donoghue* v. *Stevenson*[63] and *Rylands* v. *Fletcher,*[64] which were decided long after 1826, have been unquestioningly accepted in Singapore courts and become part of Singapore law.[65]

---

[60] See e.g. *Mah Kah Yew* v. *P.P.*, *supra*, n. 38; *The "Kota Pahlawan"* [1982] 2 M.L.J. 8 at 9-10; *Low Kok Tong* v. *Teo Chan Pan* [1982] 2 M.L.J. 299 at 301.
[61] For a thorough treatment of this topic, see A.B.L. Phang, " 'Overseas Fetters': Myth or Reality?" [1983] 2 M.L.J. cxxxix.
[62] See e.g. *K.M.A. Abdul Rahim & Anor.* v. *Owners of "Lexa Maersk" & Ors.* [1973] 2 M.L.J. 121 at 125-126; *Dobb & Co. Ltd.* v. *Hecla* [1973] 2 M.L.J. 128 at 129-130; *Hoon Wee Thim* v. *Pacific Tin Consolidated Corpn* [1966] 2 M.L.J. 240 at 249-251; *Loh Saik Pew* v. *Tan Huat Chan* [1976] 2 M.L.J. 1.
[63] [1932] A.C. 562.
[64] (1868) L.R. 3 H.L. 330.
[65] See *supra*, n. 62, the cases of *K.M.A. Abdul Rahim*, *Dobb & Co. Ltd.* and *Hoon Wee Thim*.

This practice of applying post-1826 English common law decisions appears to be based on two assumptions.[66] The first assumption is that although statute law reception under the Second Charter has a "cut-off" date (*i.e.* 1826), there is none for common law reception because the common law has always been what it now is. Under this theory, judges do not make law but merely declare it. This "declaratory" theory of the common law justifies the continuing reception of English common law decisions under the Second Charter. The second assumption is that the English common law is of universal application. Thus, English common law decisions will generally be followed *i.e.*, they are highly persuasive.

Both the above assumptions are somewhat questionable today.[67] The declaratory theory of the common law has, in recent times, fallen into serious disrepute as an antiquated legal fiction.[68] Thus, it is a questionable basis on which to apply post-1826 English common law decisions in Singapore.

As for the theory of the universality of the English common law, which emerged during the heyday of the British Empire,[69] it has been eroded somewhat in more modern times. However, to the extent that it is still adhered to, this theory places undue fetters on independent common law development. Since the Privy Council is Singapore's supreme appellate tribunal, it would be instructive to look at their Lordships' views on this matter. Although the question of permissible independent common law development has not been dealt with in the context of a Singapore appeal, the Privy Council has addressed this issue in several appeals from other jurisdictions. Such decisions are highly persuasive if not binding on Singapore courts,[70] and therefore shed important light on the permissible limits of independent common law development in Singapore.

---

[66] See G.W. Bartholomew, "The Singapore Legal System" in *Singapore: Society in Transition* (Riaz Hassan, ed. 1976), p. 90.

[67] *Id.*

[68] See e.g. P.S. Atiyah, "Judges and Policy" (1980) 15 Is. L.R. 346 at 346-347; Lord Reid, "The Judge as Law Maker" (1972) 12 Journal of the SPTL 22 at 22-23.

[69] See *e.g. Joseph Trimble* v. *George Hill* (1879) 5 App. Cas. 342, P.C.

[70] See *Fatuma binti Mohamed bin Salim Bakshuwen & Anor.* v. *Mohamed bin Salim Bakshuwen* [1952] A.C. 1. The circumstances in which Privy Council appeals from other jurisdictions are binding on Singapore courts appear to remain uncertain. For example, in *Khalid Panjang* v. *P.P., supra,* n. 39, the Federal Court (sitting in Singapore) indicated that such decisions are binding only where they deal with a statutory provision word for word the same as the corresponding provision in a local

As early as 1927, the case of *Robins* v. *National Trust Co.*, had already established that colonial courts were not bound by decisions of the English Court of Appeal.[71] The status of House of Lords' decisions, however, has remained more ambivalent.[72] In 1967, the Privy Council in *Australian Consolidated Press* v. *Uren*[73] upheld the decision of the Australian High Court which had refused to follow a House of Lords' decision on a common law matter. In doing so, their Lordships acknowledged that the common law need not necessarily be the same everywhere and that it could develop differently in different countries.[74] Their Lordships did, however, go on to say that uniformity of the common law might be more desirable in certain matters (*e.g.* commercial law) than in others (which were primarily of local concern).[75] Since *Uren,* there have been other Privy Council decisions which have shed further light on their Lordships' attitude to the independent development of the common law in different countries. Some of these decisions are not easy to reconcile with the rest. The picture that emerges from a survey of some of the decisions since *Uren* seem to suggest that, in matters which their Lordships perceive to be of largely local or domestic concern or which depend on local considerations,[76] they would be more tolerant of independent legal development. However, in matters which the Privy Council feels are of common or universal concern and divorced from local considerations (*e.g.* commercial matters), the local courts are expected to follow the English position.[77] *A fortiori,* where English law is accepted to be the applicable law, local courts are expected to follow

---

statute. In *V.C Jacob* v. *A.G.* [1970] 2 M.L.J. 133 at 136, the High Court (per Wee Chong Jin C. J.) held itself bound by a Privy Council decision on appeal from Ceylon in a common law matter (*i.e.* natural justice).However, in *Mah Kah Yew* v. *P.P.* [1971] 1 M.L.J. 1 at 3, the same court and judge appeared to suggest that only Privy Council decisions on appeal from Singapore were binding on Singapore courts.

[71] [1927] A.C. 515. See also *de Lasala* v. *de Lasala* [1979] 2 All E.R. 1146 at 1152-1153.
[72] See Phang, *supra*, n. 61 at cxlvi-cxlix.
[73] [1969] 1 A.C. 590.
[74] *Id.*, at 641.
[75] *Id.*
[76] E.g., the award of exemplary damages in libel actions (*Uren*).
[77] See e.g., *Hart* v. *O'Connor* [1985] 3 W.L.R. 214; *Tai Hing Ltd.* v. *Liu Chong Hing Bank* [1985] 3 W.L.R. 317. In *Hart,* which concerned the contractual capacity of a mentally disabled person, the Privy Council overruled the unanimous opinion of the New Zealand courts and thwarted their attempt to create a different common law rule for New Zealand on this issue. It was assumed that the English position should also prevail in New Zealand. In *Tai Hing,* it was not necessary for the Privy Council

a House of Lords' decision covering the point in issue (since that is what the Privy Council itself would do).[78]

There are, however, some cases which do not quite fit within the above analysis. For instance, *de Lasala* v. *de Lasala*,[79] seems to go to the extent of directing local courts to follow the English position (as expounded by the House of Lords) as a general rule unless the circumstances were "inappropriate."[80] The judgment in that case was written by Lord Diplock, and seems difficult to reconcile with what his Lordship said two months later when he delivered the Second Tun Abdul Razak Memorial Lecture in Malaysia. On the latter occasion, Lord Diplock acknowledged that the common law could develop differently in Malaysia and England.[81] This tolerant attitude was also reflected in the 1984 Privy Council decision of *Jamil bin Harun* v. *Yang Kamsiah*,[82] an appeal from Malaysia. In that case, the Privy Council said that it was for the Malaysian courts themselves to decide (subject to Malaysian legislation) whether to follow English case law, and that their Lordships would normally accept the Federal Court's view as to the persuasiveness of modern English case law unless the Federal Court had overlooked or misconstrued some statutory provision or committed some error of legal principle recognised and accepted in Malaysia.[83]

Thus, while it seems clear as a matter of principle that the Privy Council will tolerate a certain measure of local autonomy in developing the common law,[84] it remains unclear where the permissible limits lie. This being the situation, the application of post-1826 English common law decisions in Singapore should not be done on the basis

---

to decide whether English law was the applicable law on the issue of the extent of a customer's duty to his bank in operating a current account. This was because the parties had accepted English law as the applicable law, and the action proceeded on this assumption.

[78] See *Tai Hing Ltd, id.,* at 331.
[79] [1979] 2 All E.R. 1146.
[80] *Id.*, at 1153.
[81] Lord Diplock, "Judicial Control of Government" [1979] 2 M.L.J. cxl at cxli.
[82] [1984] 2 W.L.R. 668.
[83] *Id.*, at 672.
[84] For example, House of Lords' decisions may be departed from if they are inappropriate to local circumstances (*de Lasala*); or where custom, statute or other reasons (peculiar to the jurisdiction in question) require the Privy Council to determine whether English law is applicable in the first place (*Tai Hing Ltd., supra*, n. 77 at 331); or where the matter is of purely local concern or depends on local considerations *(Uren).*

of an automatic assumption that English common law is applicable, since even the Privy Council has recognised that there are exceptions to this theory.

English cases interpreting English statutes which have been substantially adopted in Singapore are also very persuasive, particularly where there is an absence of local decisions. Over the years, Singapore has enacted much legislation based on English models. This has been particularly true in the area of commercial law. Thus, Singapore statutes such as the Bills of Exchange Act[85] and the Banking Act[86] are substantially similar to their English counterparts. Further, section 5 of the Civil Law Act[87] provides for the continuing reception of English law governing mercantile matters, so that English commercial statutes such as the Sale of Goods Act 1979[88] and the Partnership Act 1890[89] are applicable in Singapore. One inevitable consequence of this heavy infiltration of English statutes has been that the English cases interpreting and applying them, although not binding, have generally been regarded as highly persuasive.[90] In fact, they are often applied as a matter of course. This attitude recently received support from the Privy Council in *de Lasala* and *Tai Hing Ltd.* In *de Lasala*, their Lordships directed that where the interpretation of recent local legislation modelled on English legislation was concerned, Hong Kong courts should treat themselves as being bound by the House of Lords even though, in theory, they were not.[91] In *Tai Hing Ltd.*, the Privy Council ruled that "once it was accepted that the applicable law was English, the Judicial Committee would follow a House of Lords' decision which covered the point in issue."[92] Decisions of the English Court of Appeal, however, are merely persuasive.[93]

From the foregoing, it may be seen that due to various factors (*e.g.*, Singapore's colonial heritage and the views of the Privy Council), English judicial precedents exercise a strong influence on the

---

[85] Cap. 28.
[86] Cap. 182.
[87] Cap. 30, as amended by Act No. 24 of 1979.
[88] c. 54.
[89] 53 & 54 Vict. c. 39.
[90] See e.g. *Low Kok Tong* v. *Teo Chan Pan* [1982] 2 M.L.J. 299: *Gomez nee David* v. *Gomez* [1985] 1 M.L.J. 27 at 28.
[91] *Supra*, n. 80.
[92] *Supra*, n. 78.
[93] See *de Lasala, supra*, n. 79 at 1152; Phang, *supra*, n. 61 at cxl-cxlv.

Singapore legal system, particularly as regards the development of Singapore common law, the interpretation of Singapore statutes based on English legislation and the interpretation of English law received in Singapore.

Apart from English decisions, judicial precedents from other jurisdictions may also be persuasive in certain specific areas of Singapore law. For example, Indian decisions are persuasive in the areas of criminal law and procedure because Singapore borrowed heavily from India in these areas. For the same reasons, Australian cases are persuasive in the field of company law, and Malaysian cases in the area of constitutional law.

E. Custom

The general reception of English law under the Second Charter of Justice 1826 was subject to three qualifications, one of which was that English law should be modified in its application to Singapore so as not to operate any injustice or oppression on the indigenous people. Regard was to be had to the religions, usages and manners of the people. This principle was applied primarily in family law and related matters. Thus, English law came to be modified by Chinese, Malay and Hindu customary law in these areas,[94] and likewise, some native usages or customs acquired the force of law. However, since 1961, the Women's Charter has unified family law for all ethno-religious groups except the Muslims, who are separately regulated by the Administration of Muslim Law Act.[95] Muslims in Singapore are predominantly of Malay descent.[96] Where Malay Muslims are concerned, the application of Muslim law is further modified by Malay custom as regards marriage, divorce[97] and the distribution of the estate of an intestate.[98] Thus, since 1961, Muslim customary law and the Malay custom applicable to Malay Muslims appear to be the only strands of customary or personal law which continue to have some significance in Singapore.[99]

---

[94] See *Cheang Thye Phin* v. *Tan Ah Loy* [1920] A.C 369; *Isaac Penhas* v. *Tan Soo Eng* [1953] A.C. 304.
[95] Cap. 42.
[96] See *supra*, Chapter I, n. 68.
[97] Administration of Muslim Law Act, Cap. 42, s. 35(3).
[98] *Id.*, s. 106.
[99] However, Chinese customary law may still be relevant in certain situations: see Chapter I, n. 69.

Apart from the foregoing, there are also "legal" or "trade" customs. To qualify, the custom concerned must be certain and must not be unreasonable or illegal. In Singapore, the practice of marking cheques[100] is a recognised banking custom.[101] Legal or trade customs do not have the force of law until they receive judicial recognition.

Lastly, it is appropriate to end this survey of the sources of Singapore law by noting that, as in civil law countries, academic writings are not a formal source of law. However, whereas such writings have exercised an important influence on legal development in the civil law world, they have never enjoyed the same regard in the English common law world. With the exception of a number of highly respected text-books,[102] courts generally regard academic writings as carrying little weight.

---

[100] *I.e.*, the "certifying" of cheques by bankers as good for payment at the request of the drawer.

[101] See Myint Soe, *supra*, n. 28 at pp. 29-30; M. Cheang, "Marking of Cheques: *Bank of Baroda Ltd. v. Punjab National Bank, Ltd.* [1944] A.C. 176" [1979] 1 M.L.J. xvi at xix.

[102] E.g., Snell's *Principles of Enquity*, Mayne & McGregor on Damages, Chitty on Contracts, etc.

Chapter III

The Structure of Government

A legal system does not exist in a vacuum. It reflects, and is conditioned by, the political system within which it operates. Thus, the Singapore legal system may be better understood when viewed against the political structure within which it functions.

The Republic of Singapore is a unitary state with a parliamentary system of government based on the Westminster model. The organs of state are provided for by a written constitution which forms the supreme law of the republic. The Constitution[1] lays down the structure and organisation of the three organs of the state — the executive, the legislature and the judiciary.

A. The Executive

Under the Constitution, the chief executive of Singapore is the President,[2] who is elected by Parliament for a four-year term.[3] The Constitution also provides for the post of a Vice-President[4] but none has been elected to date. Although the executive authority of Singapore is vested in the President, it is exercisable not just by him, but also by the Cabinet, or any Minister authorised by the Cabinet.[5] In reality, the President is a titular Head of State with no real executive power. Thus, the Constitution provides that, as a general principle, the President is to act on the advice of the Cabinet except in a few specified circumstances *e.g.* the appointment of the Prime Minister.[6] Although the President has discretion in appointing the Prime Minister,[7] he can only appoint as Prime Minister "a Member of Parliament who in his judgment is likely to command the confidence of the majority of the Members of Parliament."[8]

---

[1] Reprint of the Constitution of the Republic of Singapore 1980, as amended by Acts No. 24 of 1980, No. 7 of 1981, No. 16 of 1984 and No. 110 of 1985. All references to "Art/(s)." hereinafter refer to the Constitution.
[2] Art. 23(1).
[3] Art. 17(1).
[4] Art. 22.
[5] *Supra*, n. 2.
[6] Art. 21.
[7] Art. 21(2).
[8] Art. 25.

The Cabinet comprises the Prime Minister and other Ministers.[9] It is the body in which primary executive power is reposed. The Cabinet is responsible for "the general direction and control of the Government" and is collectively responsible to Parliament.[10] The Cabinet Ministers are appointed from among the Members of Parliament by the President acting on the advice of the Prime Minister.[11] Only the Prime Minister has the authority to summon the Cabinet.[12]

As regards tenure of office, the position of Prime Minister may be declared vacant if the Prime Minister resigns or if the President acting in his discretion is satisfied that the Prime Minister has ceased to command the confidence of a majority of the Members of Parliament.[13] For other Ministers, their positions become vacant when they resign or if their appointment is revoked by the President acting on the advice of the Prime Minister.[14]

The Prime Minister may charge any Minister with responsibility for any department or subject.[15] In discharging their duties and functions, Ministers may be assisted by Parliamentary Secretaries appointed for this purpose from among the Members of Parliament by the President acting on the advice of the Prime Minister.[16] In addition, the Prime Minister has power to allocate one or more Permanent Secretaries to each Ministry to exercise supervision over the department(s) to which they are allocated, subject to the general direction and control of the relevant Minister.[17]

The office of the Attorney-General is also subsumed under the heading "The Executive" in the Constitution.[18] However, in view of its important and dominantly legal functions, the Attorney-General may legitimately be regarded as a key legal institution and is therefore dealt with in Chapter IV.

---

[9] Art. 24(1).
[10] Art. 24(2).
[11] Art. 25(1).
[12] Art. 28(1).
[13] Art. 26(1).
[14] Art. 26(2).
[15] Art. 30.
[16] Art. 31.
[17] Art. 34.
[18] Art. 35(1).

B. The Legislature

1. Composition

The Singapore legislature is made up of the President and Parliament.[19] Parliament is a unicameral body composed of elected representatives. The Constitution sets out the qualifications[20] for membership of Parliament. A potential Member of Parliament must, *inter alia*, be at least 21 years of age and a Singapore citizen. Factors which disqualify a person from becoming a Member of Parliament are also set out in the Constitution.[21] For example, if he is an undischarged bankrupt, he is not eligible for parliamentary membership. The law currently provides for a total membership of 79[22] in Parliament *i.e.*, one member for each constituency. However, the legislature may, by law, change this number.[23] The details of election procedures are left to be filled in by statutes and subsidiary legislation.[24]

In 1984, the Constitution was amended to create a new class of parliamentary members — Non-Constituency Members of Parliament — to be chosen from among candidates of opposition political parties who fail to get elected into Parliament. A maximum of 3 non-constituency members with limited voting rights are to be selected from opposition candidates polling the highest percentage of votes (subject to a minimum of 15 percent of the votes in the electoral division contested).[25] One of the purposes behind this novel scheme was to satisfy a growing popular desire to see some opposition in a parliament which had been monopolised by the ruling People's Ac-

---

[19] Art. 38.
[20] Art. 44, as amended by Act No. 24 of 1980.
[21] Art. 45.
[22] Art. 39(1), as amended by Act No. 16 of 1984. See The Parliamentary Elections (Names and Boundaries of Electoral Divisions) Notification 1984, No. S. 188/84, published in the Singapore Government Gazette Subsidiary Legislation Supplement, dated 13 July 1984.
[23] See the Parliamentary Elections Act, Cap. 50, as amended by Act No. 22 of 1984, and the subsidiary legislation made thereunder.
[24] See *e.g.* The Parliamentary Elections (Posters and Banners) Regulations 1976, as amended by G.N. No. S 230/84, dated 31 August 1984; the Parliamentary Membership Act 1980, No. 25 of 1980; *supra*, nn. 22-23.
[25] See the Constitution (Amendment) Act 1984, No. 16 of 1984, s. 4, read with the Parliamentary Elections (Amendment) Act 1984, No. 22 of 1984, s. 3.

tion Party for more than 20 years.[26] It was also thought that such an arrangement would operate to strengthen Singapore's parliamentary institutions.[27]

The Constitution also stipulates that the maximum term of each elected parliament is 5 years from the date of the first sitting.[28] Thereafter, parliament is to stand dissolved and general elections for a new parliament are to be held within 3 months thereof.[29] Although Members of Parliament are generally elected for 5-year terms, parliamentary seats may automatically become vacant in certain circumstances *e.g.* where a Member of Parliament ceases to be a Singapore citizen.[30] Any such vacancies are filled by holding by-elections.[31] Parliament is to be in session at least once a year,[32] and there must not be a gap of more than 6 months between the last sitting in one session and the first sitting of the next session.[33] Parliamentary proceedings are governed by Standing Orders.[34]

2. The Legislative Process

How are statutes enacted in Singapore? The legislative process is briefly outlined below.[35]

As in Malaysia and England, a statute is first introduced into Parliament as a Bill. Bills are normally introduced by Ministers or other Members of Parliament. The Bill then goes through three readings in Parliament. The first reading occurs when the Bill is introduced into Parliament for the first time.[36] On the second reading,[37] the Minister responsible for moving the Bill usually makes a speech explaining the objects and reasons behind the Bill. A debate

---

[26] See the comments of the Prime Minister, Mr. Lee Kuan Yew, at the second reading of the Constitution of the Republic of Singapore (Amendment) Bill, Singapore Parliamentary Debates Official Report, Vol. 44, 24 July 1984, col. 1726.
[27] See *id.*, at col. 1739.
[28] Art. 65(4).
[29] Art. 66.
[30] Art. 46(2).
[31] Art. 49, as amended by Act No. 16 of 1984.
[32] Art. 64(1).
[33] *Id.*
[34] Art. 52.
[35] See Myint Soe, *The General Principles of Singapore Law* (Rev. Reprint 1982), pp. 48-50.
[36] See the Standing Orders of the Parliament of Singapore, Standing Order No. 64(2).
[37] *Id.*, Standing Order No. 67(1).

on the Bill may then ensue, since members would have had time to consider the previously circulated Bill. Sometimes, particularly in the case of controversial or important Bills, the Bill may be sent on to a Select Committee which then reports on it.[38] Next, the Bill goes through a third reading.[39] At this stage, amendments (if any) may be incorporated.[40] Then the Bill is put to the vote. The general rule is that a simple majority is sufficient.[41] However, a two-third majority is required in three situations:

(a) where the Presidential Council[42] renders an "adverse report" on a Bill, but Parliament still desires to proceed and present the Bill for the presidential assent[43];
(b) a resolution to remove the President[44] or Vice-President[45] from office;
(c) a resolution to remove the Clerk of Parliament from office.[46]

In addition, Bills which seek to amend the Constitution have to satisfy special requirements.[47]

Once the Bill is passed by Parliament, it generally has to be submitted to a non-elected advisory body called the Presidential Council for Minority Rights.[48] The Council was set up in 1970 to safeguard the rights of minority groups. Given Singapore's multiracial population and past history of communal strife, it was thought necessary to create a watchdog body to ensure that no legislation enacted by the government of the day unfairly discriminated against any minority group. The Council vets every Bill (except for three categories of Bills) to see whether it discriminates against any racial

---

[38] *Id.*, Standing Order No. 65. See *e.g.*, the Report of the Select Committee on the Criminal Procedure Code (Amendment) Bill 1976, Parl. 4 of 1976, presented to Parliament on 24 June 1976.
[39] *Id.*, Standing Order No. 72.
[40] *Id.*, Standing Order No. 71.
[41] Art. 57(1).
[42] See *infra*, for a discussion of the Presidential Council.
[43] Art. 78(6) (c).
[44] Art. 17(3).
[45] Art. 22(3).
[46] Art. 51(4).
[47] See *supra*, Chapter II.A.
[48] For an account of the history and development of this Council, see S. Jayakumar, *Constitutional Law* (1976), pp. 17-28. See also S.M. Thio, "The Presidential Council" [1969] 1 M.L.J. xli; essays by Thio, Marshall, Khoo and de Cruz in (1969) Singapore Law Review, pp. 1-25.

or religious community[49] *i.e.*, whether it is a "differentiating measure."[50] The Council is given 30 days[51] to study the Bill and report on whether it contains any such measures. Where the Council reports that a Bill contains such a defect, the report is an "adverse report." Where the Council makes a favourable report (*i.e.*, that the Bill contains no differentiating measures) or where it makes no report within the time prescribed (in which case, the Bill is conclusively presumed not to contain any differentiating measures[52]), the Bill is next presented to the President for his assent. Thereupon, the Bill finally becomes an Act of Parliament *i.e.*, law.[53]

However, if the Council submits an adverse report, Parliament can do one of two things: first, Parliament can make the necessary amendments to the Bill and re-submit it to the Council for approval; alternatively, Parliament could decide to proceed to present the Bill for the President's assent in spite of the adverse report. The latter course of action can only be adopted if a motion for such action has been passed by the affirmative vote of at least two-thirds of the total parliamentary membership.[54]

As briefly mentioned earlier, three types of Bills are exempted from undergoing the Council vetting[55] outlined above. They are: "Money Bills,"[56] urgent Bills, and Bills affecting defence, security, public safety, peace or good order in Singapore.

From the foregoing, it may be seen that although the Constitution states that legislature comprises the President and Parliament,[57] and that legislative authority is exercised through Bills passed by Parliament and assented to by the President,[58] the Presidential Council, though not part of Parliament, nevertheless has an important role in the legislative process because all Bills (except for the three categories mentioned above) must be submitted to the Council for its report

---

[49] Art. 77.
[50] Art. 68.
[51] Under certain circumstances, this period may be extended by the Speaker of Parliament at the Council's request: see art. 78(4).
[52] Art. 78(5).
[53] Art. 58.
[54] Art. 78(6) (c).
[55] Art. 78(7).
[56] For the definition of "Money Bill", see arts. 68 and 78(8).
[57] Art. 38.
[58] Art. 58.

Structure of Government 47

before they can be presented for the presidential assent.[59]

Finally, it is important to note that a Bill does not necessarily come into force upon its enactment as a statute. Instead, an Act often comes into operation only on the date of its publication in the Gazette.[60]

The topic of legislation leads naturally into that of subsidiary legislation.[61] Time and other practical contraints have made it an increasingly widespread practice for legislatures to lay down broad principles of law in statutes, leaving the details to be filled in by ministers and other administrative officers or agencies via "subsidiary legislation."[62] However, because of the danger of abuse of power in granting administrative agencies powers to make rules and regulations, there is the need to exercise control over subsidiary legislation. The subsidiary legislative process is thus subject to both procedural and substantive safeguards in the shape of the *ultra vires* rule. Accordingly, subsidiary legislation must be made pursuant to the procedure prescribed by the parent Act.[63] This procedure may vary from Act to Act. Thus, some Acts merely state that a certain person or body is empowered to make rules or regulations thereunder, and do not prescribe any specific procedure.[64] Other Acts go further and stipulate that such rules or regulations must be published in the Gazette.[65] Still others go even further and require the rules or regulations to be presented to Parliament for its sanction.[66] Unless otherwise expressly provided in any Act, subsidiary legislation generally has to be published in the Government Gazette, and (unless such subsidiary legislation provides otherwise) normally takes effect on the date of such publication.[67] Subsidiary legislation is also subject to substantive restrictions *i.e.*, it cannot be inconsistent with or exceed the scope or authority conferred by the parent Act.[68] Both legislation

---

[59] See Jayakumar, *supra*, n. 48 at p. 18.
[60] See art. 58(2). For example, the Small Claims Tribunals Act 1984, No. 27 of 1984, was brought into operation on 15 January 1985 by G.N. No. S 18/85 dated 9 January 1985.
[61] See *supra*, Chapter II, n. 20.
[62] Also known as subordinate or delegated legislation.
[63] See Myint Soe, *supra*, n. 35 at pp. 51-52.
[64] See *e.g.* the Companies Act, Cap. 185. Reprint 1985, s. 411.
[65] See *e.g.* the Estate Duty Act, Cap. 137, s. 49; Interpretation Act, Cap. 3, s. 23.
[66] See *e.g.* Women's Charter, Cap. 47, Reprint 1981, s. 165(2).
[67] Interpretation Act, Cap. 3, s. 23(1).
[68] See *id.*, s. 19(c).

and subsidiary legislation are also constrained by the principle of constitutional supremacy.[69]

C. The Judiciary

The third organ of state is the judiciary. The Constitution vests judicial power in the Supreme Court and in such subordinate courts as may be provided by any written law for the time being in force.[70] It also provides for appeals from this judicial hierarchy to the Judicial Committee of the Privy Council which sits in London.[71] Most of the constitutional provisions on the judiciary relate to Supreme Court judges; more specifically, their qualifications, appointment, tenure of office and remuneration. These provisions reflect a concern on the part of the framers of the Constitution to ensure independence of the judiciary. The details of the structure, jurisdiction and powers of the courts are mainly provided for by the Supreme Court of Judicature Act[72] and the Subordinate Courts Act.[73] The Singapore judicial system is dealt with in further detail in the following chapter.

---

[69] See art. 4 and M.P. Jain, *Administrative Law of Malaysia and Singapore* (1980), pp. 66-67. Note, however, that the Constitution is, in fact, quite flexible *i.e.*, it is relatively easy to amend: see *supra*, Chapter II.A.
[70] Art. 93.
[71] Art. 100.
[72] Cap. 15, as amended by Acts No. 58 of 1973, No. 10 of 1978 and No. 4 of 1986.
[73] Cap. 14, as amended by Acts No. 34 of 1973, No. 6 of 1976 and No. 3 of 1986.

Chapter IV

Legal Institutions

This chapter describes the structure and role of the key legal institutions in Singapore *viz.* the judicial system, the legal profession, the office of the Attorney-General, the Legal Service and some of the major law enforcement agencies.

A. The Judicial System

The Singapore Judicial System

```
                 Judicial Committee
                 of the Privy Council
                         |
     ┌───────────────────┴──────────────┐
  Court of Appeal              Court of Criminal
     |                              Appeal        ┌─ Supreme
     |                                            |  Court
     └──────────────┬───────────────┘             |
                    |                             |
                High Court  ────────────────── ──┘
                    |
  ┌─────────┬─────────┬─────────┬─────────┬─────────┐
District  Magistrates' Juvenile  Coroners'  Small Claims
Courts    Courts       Courts    Courts     Tribunals
```

Subordinate Courts

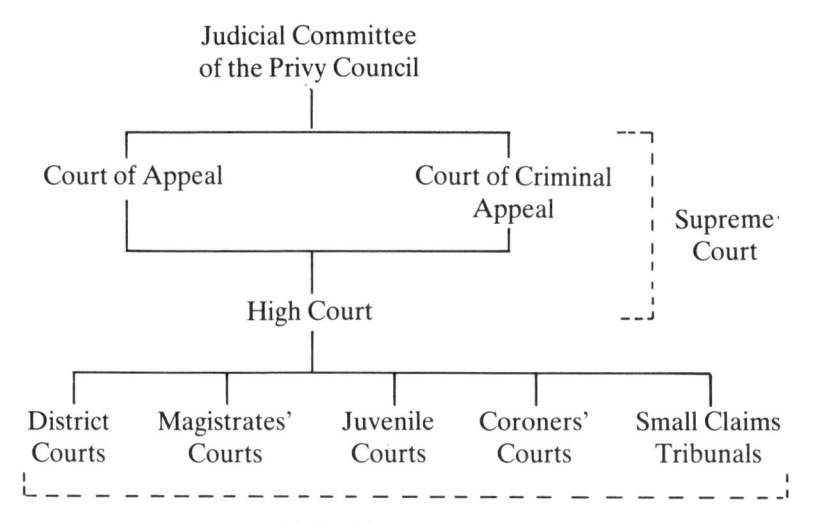

Courts are tribunals which exercise jurisdiction over persons by reason of the sanction of the law.[1] The Singapore judicial system comprises three tiers of courts: the Subordinate Courts at the bottom, the Supreme Court in the middle and the Judicial Committee of the Privy Council at the apex of the hierarchy. Before we look at each of these tiers in greater detail, a few general comments are in order.

The present judicial system essentially preserves the English-style judicial system evolved during the colonial era. This may be seen in the fact that most of the courts (*e.g.* the Supreme Court and the

---

[1] *Halsbury's* Laws of England (4th ed. 1973), Vol. 10, p. 313 para. 701.

District Courts) still retain their old names,[2] and perform functions broadly similar to those they had in colonial days. Like courts in other common law countries, Singapore courts have jurisdiction[3] to deal with both civil and criminal matters as well as public law disputes (*i.e.*, disputes involving a government agency). By contrast, apart from criminal matters, the jurisdiction of the ordinary courts in most civil law systems is basically confined to "private law" disputes.[4] In such systems, administrative law disputes are generally dealt with by a separate system of administrative courts[5] which also apply a body of administrative law distinct from the law administered in the ordinary civil law courts.[6]

Although Singapore does not have a separate system of administrative courts in the continental sense, there are special tribunals with power to entertain specific types of administrative disputes. For instance, there is an Industrial Arbitration Court which deals purely with employer-employee disputes; a Land Acquisition Appeals Board which entertains appeals arising from government acquisition of land; and a Rent Conciliation Board which decides disputes relating to rent control. Other special administrative tribunals include the Board of Review (Income Tax) and the Valuation Review Board (Property Tax).[7] For the purposes of describing the Singapore judicial system, the writer will focus only on the ordinary courts which exercise civil and/or criminal jurisdiction. Needless to say, in a work of this nature, it is not possible to be comprehensive. Thus, the following account only sketches out the more prominent features of the Singapore judicial system.

1. The Judicial Committee of the Privy Council

Although it sits in England, the Judicial Committee of the Privy Council is the highest appellate court in the Singapore judicial sys-

---

[2] See R. Braddell, *The Law of the Straits Settlements: A Commentary* (3rd ed. 1982), pp. 121-123.
[3] "Jurisdiction" refers to the legal authority of the court to deal with the disputes brought before it. See *infra*, Chapter IV.A.2.
[4] See R.B. Schlesinger, *Comparative Law: Cases-Text-Materials* (4th ed. 1980), p. 462. As used in contrast to "public law", "private law" refers to the law governing relationships between private individuals.
[5] *Id.*, pp. 463-464.
[6] *Id.*, pp. 479-480.
[7] See Myint Soe, *The General Principles of Singapore Law* (Rev. Rep. 1982), p. 72.

Legal Institutions 51

tem. This has been the position since colonial days.[8] The jurisdiction of this body developed from the traditional notion that the British sovereign was the fountainhead of justice and therefore had a prerogative right, as well as a duty, to entertain appeals from the courts in his dominions.[9] Appeals from the colonies therefore lay to the King in Council.[10] The British sovereign traditionally exercised this appellate jurisdiction through the Privy Council, the body of personal advisers to the Crown. In its earlier stages of development, the Privy Council's functions were more administrative and political than judicial.[11] However, as the British empire expanded, especially in the eighteenth and nineteenth centuries, the volume of the Privy Council's legal business increased correspondingly so that, by 1833, the Privy Council's appellate jurisdiction came to be exercised by a special Judicial Committee of the Privy Council, staffed only by trained lawyers.[12]

During the heyday of the British empire, the Judicial Committee of the Privy Council was the highest appellate court for Britain's many colonies and possessions around the world. However, the jurisdiction of the Privy Council[13] suffered a sharp decline in the post-Second World War era when many British colonies (among them India and Pakistan) attained independence and ceased to retain the Privy Council as their court of last resort.[14] Some other countries, however, opted for a more gradual mode of abolishing Privy Council appeals.[15] Just recently, Malaysia took the final step in phasing out

---

[8] See *supra*, Chapter I.B.
[9] See *R.* v. *Bertrand* (1867) L.R. 1 P.C. 520 at 530; see also *Fryer* v. *Barnard* (1724) 2 P.W. 262; L.P. Beth, "The Judicial Committee: Its Development, Organisation and Procedure" (1975) 3 Pub L. 219.
[10] See e.g., Braddell, *supra*, n. 2 at p. 13.
[11] See Beth, *supra*, n. 9 at pp. 220-221.
[12] *Id.*, pp. 221-223.
[13] In legal circles, the Judicial Committee of the Privy Council is commonly referred to as the "Privy Council" for the sake of brevity. However, it must be remembered that it is the *Judicial Committee* of the Privy Council that is being referred to, and not the Privy Council generally. Strictly speaking, the latter term would include the bigger body of mainly non-judicial members. Thus, the term "Privy Council" as used hereinafter refers to the Judicial Committee of the Privy Council.
[14] E.M. Campbell, "The Decline of the Jurisdiction of the Judicial Committee of the Privy Council" (1959) 33 A.L.J. 196.
[15] E.g., Australia: see A.R. Blackshield, "The Last of England — Farewell to Their Lordships Forever" Law Institute Journal (Vict.), Oct. 1982, Vol. 56 #10, 780. Australia finally abolished Privy Council appeals completely in March 1986: see *The Straits Times*, 3 March 1986.

Privy Council appeals completely.[16] By contrast, Singapore has, to date, made no attempts to abolish appeals to the Privy Council. Some observers, particularly foreign ones, have commented that the retention of the Privy Council as court of last resort seems incongruous with the status of sovereign nationhood. Why then does Singapore continue to retain the Privy Council as its highest appellate court?

In 1967,[17] the Prime Minister expressed the opinion that there would be "a higher degree of confidence in the integrity of our judicial process" if the government was "wise enough to leave alone the rights of appeal to some superior body outside Singapore." He indicated that this was especially important from the viewpoint of encouraging commerce. He also said that he saw "no credit in our trying to run a close circuit judicial system as our own." To the writer's knowledge, the issue of retaining Privy Council appeals has not been publicly considered since then. Presumably, the rationale behind the original decision to retain Privy Council appeals still holds true today. In addition, a new problem has been identified in recent years, which tends to lend support to the continued retention of Privy Council appeals. This is the shortage of High Court judges. In 1981, the Prime Minister highlighted the difficulty in recruiting suitable candidates for the High Court bench. He even indicated that if this problem persisted in the next few years, expatriate lawyers would be considered.[18] Since the difficulty in recruiting High Court judges remains a problem today,[19] it is highly unlikely that Privy Council appeals will be abolished in the near future as this would only exacerbate the shortage of higher court judges servicing the judicial system. Thus, the reasons why Singapore continues to retain Privy Council appeals are perhaps best summed up in the words of Lord Normand: "[T]he continuance of the appeal or its abolition ... is a question of convenience and not one of fundamental importance."[20]

---

[16] Privy Council appeals have been completely abolished with effect from 1 January 1985: see the Constitution (Amendment) Act 1983, No. A566 of 1983, s. 17, implemented by PU(B) 589/84; and the Courts of Judicature (Amendment) Act 1984, No. A600 of 1984, s. 2.
[17] See Singapore Parliamentary Debates Official Report, (1966-1967) Vol. 25, cols. 1294-1295.
[18] See *id.*, Vol. 40, cols. 695-697.
[19] See *id.*, Vol. 46, col. 718, per Prof. S. Jayakumar (Second Minister for Law).
[20] Lord Normand, "The Judicial Committee of the Privy Council — Retrospect and Prospect" (1950) Current Legal Problems 1 at 5.

Article 100 of the Constitution[21] read together with the Judicial Committee Act[22] permit appeals from the Court of Appeal and the Court of Criminal Appeal to lie to the Privy Council. A U.K. Order in Council[23] empowers the Privy Council to continue to hear such appeals. However, some aspects of the traditional appellate procedure of the Privy Council have had to be cosmetically modified to take account of the fact that Singapore is no longer a British colony. Two illustrations follow. In colonial days, appeals from Singapore had lain to the King in Council.[24] Today, appeals from independent Singapore are made directly to the Judicial Committee itself, and no longer to the British sovereign.[25] Also, during the colonial era, judgments of the Privy Council were traditionally cast in the form of "advice" to the British sovereign.[26] This was because of the historical origins of the Privy Council as the King's Cabinet. As a matter of convention, the sovereign then gave effect to the Privy Council's advice by way of an Order in Council adopting the advice as the judgment of the King in Council.[27] Today, when the Privy Council entertains an appeal from Singapore, its judgment takes the form of an order signed by the Registrar of the Privy Council.[28] However, apart from these token changes, most of the rules regulating the proceedings of the Judicial Committee of the Privy Council remain undisturbed.[29]

The Privy Council's non-judicial origins also partly explain why the Privy Council, unlike the House of Lords and other English judicial tribunals, adopted a single judgment procedure for centuries.[30] This practice originated from certain seventeenth century Orders (governing the proceedings of the Privy Council and its committees)

---

[21] Reprint of the Constitution of the Republic of Singapore 1980.
[22] Cap. 8.
[23] Republic of Singapore (Appeals to Judicial Committee) Order 1966, S.I. 1966 No. 1182 (made under the Singapore Act 1966, s. 3).
[24] This arrangement began with the granting of the Second Charter in 1826: see Braddell, *supra*, n. 2, at pp. 13, 27.
[25] *Supra*, n. 18, Second Schedule.
[26] See Campbell, *supra*, n. 14 at pp. 197-198; M. Nash, "Functions and Future of the Judicial Committee of the Privy Council" (1974) 124 New L.J. 1171; W.R. Anson, *The Law and Custom of the Constitution* (4th ed. 1935), p. 328.
[27] *Id.*
[28] See *Atkin's* Encyclopaedia of Court Forms (2nd ed.), pp. 232-233, Form 31.
[29] See Judicial Committee Act, Cap. 8, s. 6.
[30] See D.B. Swinfen, "The Single Judgment in the Privy Council 1833-1966" (1975) Jurid. Rev. 153.

which prohibited the publication of dissenting opinions.[31] The practice was continued over the centuries for policy reasons that do not concern us here.[32] However, in 1966,[33] this well-established procedure was changed to allow for the expression of dissenting opinions. Among the reasons for the change was the general feeling that suppression of dissenting opinions was not appropriate for what had long been accepted as a full-fledged judicial tribunal.[34] Thus, at present, Privy Council judgments contain a majority judgment, with a separate dissenting opinion where one exists. This is similar to the practice of the U.S. Supreme Court but different from that of the English House of Lords and Court of Appeal where *seriatim* judgments are the general rule.[35]

As the ultimate appellate court for several Commonwealth countries and the few remaining British colonies that still retain Privy Council appeals, the membership of the Privy Council is not confined to English judges. In fact, it has for a long time been open to prominent Commonwealth judges as well.[36] Since the turn of the century, several prominent Indian, Australian and Canadian judges have served in the Privy Council from time to time.

Against this general background information on the Privy Council, we can proceed to briefly consider when its appellate jurisdiction may be invoked. The Privy Council only entertains appeals from the Court of Appeal and the Court of Criminal Appeal.[37] In order to bring an appeal before the Privy Council, a litigant must first be able to satisfy the conditions of appeal prescribed in sections 3 and 4 of the Judicial Committee Act.[38] In civil appeals, the Court of Appeal must first have granted leave to appeal to the Privy Council.[39] Generally, such leave is normally granted as a matter of course in the case of final judgments involving sums of at least $5,000, or where the case is

---

[31] *Id.*
[32] *Id.*, p. 154 *et seq.*
[33] By virtue of the Judicial Committee (Dissenting Opinions) Order, S.I. 1966, Part I, p. 1100.
[34] See *supra*, n. 30 at p. 175.
[35] *Id.*
[36] See Beth, *supra*, n. 9 at pp. 224-225; K. Roberts-Wray, *Commonwealth and Colonial Law* (1966), p. 434.
[37] Judicial Committee Act, Cap. 8, ss. 2-3. It also hears appeals from "show cause" proceedings tried by three High Court judges under s. 98(6) of the Legal Profession Act, Cap. 217, Reprint 1982: see *infra*, Chapter IV.B.2.
[38] Cap. 8.
[39] *Id.*, s. 3(1).

from its nature a fit one for appeal.[40] However, no minimum value is prescribed for two other categories of appeals: (a) an appeal from any interlocutory judgment which the Court of Appeal considers a fit one for appeal; and (b) an appeal from any decision made by the Court of Appeal in the exercise of any original or advisory jurisdiction conferred upon it.[41]

In the residual civil appeals not covered by section 3(1) of the Judicial Committee Act, in civil appeals where the leave of the Court of Appeal was not duly obtained, and in all criminal appeals, special leave to appeal must be sought from the Privy Council itself.[42] As a practice, the Privy Council generally does not grant special leave in civil appeals unless the case raises "a far-reaching question of law or matters of dominant public importance."[43] Similarly, in criminal cases, the Privy Council ordinarily does not grant special leave to appeal unless the questions raised are of "great and general importance" and likely to recur often or where "substantial and grave injustice" has occurred as a result of some violation of the principles of natural justice or the forms of legal process.[44] It will generally refuse to interfere with the facts and evidence found by the lower courts.[45]

2. The Supreme Court

The Constitution[46] and the Supreme Court of Judicature Act[47] together provide for the existence of the Supreme Court. The Supreme Court is a superior court whereas the subordinate courts are inferior courts. Inferior courts are so called because they are generally subject to the control and supervision of superior courts.[48] The main distinction between superior and inferior courts is found in the area of jurisdiction. "Jurisdiction" refers to the authority which a

---

[40] *Id.*, s. 3(1) (a).
[41] *Id.*, s. 3(1) (b) and (c).
[42] *Id.*, s. 3(2).
[43] *Halsbury's* Laws of England (4th ed. 1973), Vol. 10, p. 366, para. 785.
[44] *Id.*, p. 367, para. 786.
[45] See *e.g., Lim Yam Teck* v. *P.P.* [1972] 2 M.L.J. 41, per Lord Kilbrandon. For a discussion by the writer of Privy Council treatment of appeals from Singapore and Malaysia since 1957, see "The Privy Council as Court of Last Resort in Singapore and Malaysia: 1957-1983" in *The Common Law in Singapore and Malaysia* (A.J. Harding ed. 1985), pp. 77-114.
[46] Art. 93.
[47] Cap. 15, s. 3.
[48] *Halsbury's* Laws of England (4th ed. 1973), Vol. 10, p. 321, para. 711.

court has to decide matters that are litigated before it or to take cognisance of matters presented in a formal way for its decision.[49]

Prima facie, no matter is deemed to be beyond the jurisdiction of a superior court unless it is expressly shown to be so, while nothing is within the jurisdiction of an inferior court unless it is expressly shown on the face of the proceedings that the particular matter is within the cognisance of the particular court.[50]

The jurisdiction of inferior courts is generally limited to causes of action within prescribed bounds or to actions where the amount claimed falls below a certain specified limit.[51] By contrast, the High Court, as a superior court, has universal (*i.e.* unlimited) jurisdiction.[52]

The Supreme Court consists of the Chief Justice and the judges of the Supreme Court.[53] It has three divisions, namely the High Court, the Court of Appeal and the Court of Criminal Appeal.[54] The High Court exercises original and appellate jurisdiction in both criminal and civil matters. However, the Court of Appeal and the Court of Criminal Appeal only have appellate jurisdiction in civil and criminal matters respectively. Since Supreme Court judges sit in all three divisions of the Supreme Court, the popular term "High Court Judge" is misleading because, technically, there is no such appointment.[55] Before we look at the three divisions in greater detail, we will consider the appointment of Supreme Court judges and the concept of independence of the judiciary.

The Appointment of Supreme Court Judges

The qualifications which a Supreme Court judge must possess are laid down in Article 96 of the Constitution. In order to qualify for appointment as a Supreme Court judge, a person must have been, for at least ten years, a "qualified person" within the meaning of section

---

[49] *Id.*, p. 323, para. 715.
[50] *Id.*, pp. 321-322, para. 713, cited with approval in *Abdul Wahab Bin Sulaiman* v. *Commandant, Tanglin Detention Barracks* [1985] 1 M.L.J. 418 at 419, per Sinnathuray J.
[51] *Halsbury's* Laws of England, *supra*, n. 48 at p. 321, para. 712.
[52] However, the High Court has no jurisdiction over matters within the jurisdiction of the Shariah Court: see *infra*, Chapter IV.A.2.a. (i).
[53] Supreme Court of Judicature Act, Cap. 15 (hereinafter "S.C.J.A."), s. 4(1).
[54] *Id.*, s. 7.
[55] See Myint Soe, *supra*, n. 7 at p. 75.

Legal Institutions

2 of the Legal Professional Act,[56] or a member of the Singapore Legal Service, or both. The Constitution envisages three types of Supreme Court judges — those appointed in the normal fashion,[57] designated judges[58] and Judicial Commissioners.[59] The qualifications and method of appointment for each of these positions are largely the same, but the tenure of office is different. Only Supreme Court judges in the first category have security of tenure *i.e.*, they are entitled to hold office till the age of 65.[60] If they are reappointed after retirement, they become designated judges. Both designated judges[61] and Judicial Commissioners[62] serve for fixed terms.

All three types of Supreme Court judges are appointed in the same way *i.e.*, they are appointed by the President acting on the advice of the Prime Minister who consults the Chief Justice for this purpose.[63] The Chief Justice himself is appointed by the President acting on the advice of the Prime Minister.[64] At present, there are altogether eight Supreme Court judges (including the Chief Justice), some of whom are designated judges. No Judicial Commissioners have yet been appointed.

The Independence of the Judiciary

The independence of the judiciary is one of the fundamental assumptions underlying the Singapore legal system. The rationale behind this concept is that justice must be objectively dispensed in the courts and that the public should have confidence in the integrity and impartiality of the courts. Judges should feel free to decide cases according to the law and their convictions, without being answerable to either the executive or the legislature. The judiciary must therefore be insulated from undue influence and be autonomous within its own field because independence of the judiciary produces justice.[65]

---

[56] Cap. 217, Reprint 1982. For an explanation of this term, see *infra*, Chapter IV.B.1.(a).
[57] Art. 95.
[58] Art. 94(3).
[59] Art. 94(4).
[60] Art. 98(1).
[61] Art. 94(3).
[62] Art. 94(4).
[63] Art. 95(2).
[64] Art. 95(1).
[65] See Lord Elwyn-Jones, "Independence of the Judiciary" [1976] 1 M.L.J. viii.

Several provisions in the Constitution are designed to secure the independence of the judiciary. For example, the concept of the separation of powers has been written into the Constitution so that executive, legislative and judicial power are exercised by three separate branches of government.[66] Also, a Supreme Court judge appointed in the ordinary way (*i.e.*, not as a designated judge or a Judicial Commissioner) has security of tenure. Once appointed, he is entitled to hold office till 65.[67] His position cannot be abolished during his continuance in office.[68] Neither can he be removed from office except by way of a very stringent procedure.[69] By contrast, designated judges, Judicial Commissioners and subordinate court judges do not enjoy security of tenure, and are akin to public servants who hold office at the President's pleasure.[70] The remuneration[71] and other terms of office[72] of Supreme Court judges are also provided for by Parliament and cannot be altered to their disadvantage after their appointment.[73] Further, Supreme Court judges are immune from liability for acts done in the discharge of their judicial duty.[74] Lastly, their conduct cannot be discussed in Parliament unless there is a substantive motion of which notice has been given by at least one-quarter of the total number of Members of Parliament.[75] Outside Parliament, the conduct of a Supreme Court judge is discussable within limits. It may not be criticised except in good faith. Criticism which is unwarranted or discourteous or insulting may amount to contempt of court which is punishable under the Supreme Court of Judicature Act.[76]

a. *The High Court*

The High Court is the lower division of the Supreme Court. It exercises both original and appellate jurisdiction in civil and criminal

---

[66] See Parts V, VI and VIII of the Constitution respectively.
[67] Art. 98(1).
[68] Art. 94(2).
[69] Art. 98.
[70] See arts. 94(3) and (4), 102(1) and 104.
[71] Art. 98(6). Such remuneration is charged on the Consolidated Fund. See also the Judges Remuneration Act, Cap. 7.
[72] Art. 98(7).
[73] Art. 98(8).
[74] S.C.J.A., s. 79. This privilege extends to subordinate court judges too: see the Subordinate Courts Act, Cap. 14 (hereinafter "S.C.A."), s. 68.
[75] Art. 99.
[76] s. 8.

matters. This means that it has power to try cases itself as well as power to hear appeals from trial courts (such as the District Courts and the Magistrates' Courts) lower down in the hierarchy, in both civil and criminal matters. As a general rule, all proceedings in the High Court (whether original or appellate) are disposed of before a single judge. This contrasts with the general civilian preference for a collegial bench.[77] However, where appeals are concerned, there may be more than one judge in cases of uncommon importance or where the law so requires.[78]

The original jurisdiction of the High Court will be looked at first. The High Court is the only trial court of general jurisdiction[79] *i.e.*, it is the only trial court in Singapore with authority to try all civil and criminal cases. The other trial courts are all subordinate courts which have limited or special jurisdiction to try civil and criminal cases. As applied to jurisdiction, the terms "general" and "special" refer to the difference between a legal authority covering the whole of a particular subject, and one limited to a part of it.[80] Courts with limited or special jurisdiction only have authority to deal with a particular class of cases, or cases where the amount in dispute falls below a prescribed sum.

(i) Original Civil Jurisdiction

Sections 16 and 17 of the Supreme Court of Judicature Act spell out the scope of the High Court's original civil jurisdiction. The High Court has specific jurisdiction in the matters enumerated in section 17. These include divorce and matrimonial causes, admiralty matters, and matters relating to wills and intestacy. In such matters, the High Court has exclusive jurisdiction. Except for civil proceedings falling within the jurisdiction of the Shariah Court,[81] the High Court has unlimited jurisdiction in all kinds of civil and criminal matters. Unlike subordinate courts such as the District and Magistrates' Courts, there

---

[77] See K. Zweigert and H. Kotz, *An Introduction to Comparative Law: Vol. I: The Framework* (1977), pp. 115-116; F.H. Lawson, A.E. Anton and L. Neville Brown, *Amos and Walton's Introduction to French Law* (3rd ed. 1979), p. 8. Thus, in France, the *tribunaux de grande instance*, which are the principal courts of first instance, are generally staffed by a collegial bench.
[78] S.C.J.A., ss. 10(1), 19 and 21(2).
[79] See the definition of "general jurisdiction" in *Black's* Law Dictionary (5th ed. 1979), p. 616.
[80] *Id.*
[81] Constituted under the Administration of Muslim Law Act, Cap. 42.

60			Singapore Legal System

is no monetary restriction on the original civil jurisdiction of the High Court. Since the civil jurisdiction of the Magistrate's Court is limited to $10,000,[82] and that of the District Court to $50,000,[83] disputes involving more than $50,000 must necessarily be tried by the High Court. Although the High Court has power to try disputes involving a smaller a sum, it ordinarily does not do so. In any case, litigants in such cases generally prefer the less expensive and more expeditious proceedings in the subordinate courts.

(ii) Original Criminal Jurisdiction

The original criminal jurisdiction of the High Court is spelt out by section 15 of the Supreme Court of Judicature Act and section 9 of the Criminal Procedure Code.[84] Under section 15, the High Court has power to try any offence committed:

(a) within Singapore; or

(b) on the high seas on board a Singapore-registered ship or aircraft; or

(c) on the high seas or any aircraft by a Singapore citizen; or

(d) by any person where the offence is piracy under international law; or

(e) by any person within or outside Singapore where the offence is punishable under the Hijacking and Protection of Aircraft Act 1978.[85]

Under section 9 of the Criminal Procedure Code, the High Court has power to try all offences under Singapore law although other courts may also have jurisdiction to try certain types of offences. Thus, as in civil matters, the High Court has general jurisdiction in criminal matters. In practice, however, the High Court normally tries only those cases falling outside the jurisdiction of the District Courts. Be that as it may, the High Court does occasionally try cases ordinarily triable in the District or Magistrates' Courts if they are unusually important.[86] The High Court has power to pass any sentence allowed

---

[82] S.C.A., s. 52, as amended by Act No. 3 of 1986.
[83] *Id.*, s. 21.
[84] Cap. 113, Reprint 1980.
[85] No. 9 of 1978.
[86] See, for example, the case of *T.T. Rajah* v. *Regina* [1963] M.L.J. 281.

by law.[87] In this sense, its sentencing powers are unlimited, unlike those of the subordinate courts.

(iii) Appellate Civil Jurisdiction

The appellate civil jurisdiction of the High Court is provided for by section 20 of the Supreme Court of Judicature Act. It consists mainly of hearing appeals from the District and Magistrates' Courts although the High Court can also hear appeals from other tribunals if any law so provides. Thus, for example, under the Workmen's Compensation Act,[88] appeals on points of law from a decision of an arbitrator in a claim for workmen's compensation lie to the High Court exercising its appellate jurisdiction. Appeals to the High Court exercising its appellate civil jurisdiction are by way of rehearing.[89] This means that the evidence may be reviewed, and further evidence may, if necessary, be adduced, although in practice this is rarely necessary.

As with its original jurisdiction in civil and criminal matters, the High Court's appellate jurisdiction is unrestricted. Thus, although appeals from the District and Magistrates' Courts only lie to the High Court as of right where the amount exceeds $2,000, the High Court may nevertheless give leave to appeal where a lesser sum is involved.[90] In hearing civil appeals, the High Court has the same powers as the Court of Appeal when the latter entertains appeals from the High Court.[91]

(iv) Appellate Criminal Jurisdiction

The appellate criminal jurisdiction of the High Court is provided for by section 19 of the Supreme Court of Judicature Act. It consists mainly of hearing appeals from District and Magistrates' Courts. It also includes hearing points of law reserved by special cases submitted by a District or Magistrate's Court. In practice, however, District and Magistrates' Courts seldom submit special cases to the High Court.[92]

---

[87] S.C.J.A., s. 15(2).
[88] No. 25 of 1975, s. 29.
[89] S.C.J.A., s. 22.
[90] *Id.*, s. 21(1), as amended by Act. No. 4 of 1986, which was bought into force on 1 March 1986 by G.N. No. S 44/86.
[91] *Supra*, n. 89. See *infra* Chapter IV.A.2b.
[92] See Myint Soe, *supra*, n. 7 at p. 78.

In hearing a criminal appeal, the High Court has power to dismiss the appeal, or reverse the judgment or order, or alter the length or nature of the sentence, or order a re-trial, or order further evidence to be taken.[93] However, the High Court cannot set aside or reverse any judgment, sentence or order of a District or Magistrate's Court unless it is satisfied that the judgment, acquittal, sentence or order was "either wrong in law or against the weight of the evidence, or in the case of a sentence, manifestly excessive or inadequate in the circumstances of the case."[94]

(v) Supervisory and Revisionary Jurisdiction

In addition to its original and appellate jurisdiction, the High Court has revisionary jurisdiction over civil and criminal proceedings in the subordinate courts.[95] This means that the High Court has power to call for the records of proceedings before any subordinate court in order to satisfy itself "as to the correctness, legality or propriety of any decision recorded or passed" in a civil proceeding[96] and "any finding, sentence or order recorded or passed" in a criminal proceeding.[97] The High Court may also investigate the regularity of any subordinate court proceedings.[98]

Theoretically, the High Court can exercise its revisionary power either at the instance of one of the parties or on its own motion. In practice, however, the latter is rarely done.[99] In civil proceedings, there is no revision at the instance of a party who could have appealed.[100] In criminal proceedings, it appears that a party may still apply for revision even though the deadline for lodging an appeal has lapsed. In exercising its powers of revision over criminal proceedings in a subordinate court, the High Court enjoys powers similar to what it has when exercising its appellate criminal jurisdiction except that it may not convert a finding of acquittal into one of conviction.[101] In the case of civil proceedings, the High Court has power to give any orders

---

[93] Criminal Procedure Code (hereinafter "C.P.C."), Cap. 113, Reprint 1980, ss. 255-256.
[94] *Id.*, s. 260.
[95] S.C.J.A., ss. 23-24.
[96] *Id.*, s. 24.
[97] *Id.*, s. 23 and C.P.C., s. 265(1).
[98] S.C.J.A., s. 24 and C.P.C., s. 265(1).
[99] See Myint Soe, *supra*, n. 7 at p. 79.
[100] S.C.J.A., s. 26.
[101] See C.P.C., s. 267.

which seem necessary to secure that substantial justice is done.[102]

Section 27 of the Supreme Court of Judicature Act augments the High Court's revisionary jurisdiction with a more general supervisory jurisdiction over all subordinate courts. This provision empowers the High Court, in the interests of justice, either at the instance of any interested party or on its own accord, to call for the record of any subordinate court proceedings at any stage of such proceedings, and either transfer the case to the High Court or give the relevant subordinate court directions for the further conduct of the case. Thus, it may be seen that the High Court's revisionary and supervisory jurisdiction appear to overlap. Be that as it may, the general intention behind them is clearly to ensure adequate control and supervision of the inferior courts by the High Court as a superior court. It is worth noting that only the High Court has powers of revision and supervision over the subordinate courts. Neither the Court of Appeal nor the Court of Criminal Appeal has such powers.

Lastly, it should be noted that when the High Court exercises its powers of revision and supervision, the parties generally have no right to be heard.[103] However, the High Court is not permitted to make a final order that prejudices any person unless that person has first had an opportunity to be heard.[104] This accords with the fundamental rules of natural justice.

b. *The Court of Appeal*

The Court of Appeal is the highest civil court sitting in Singapore. It only has appellate civil jurisdiction, and hears appeals from decisions of the High Court acting in its original and appellate civil jurisdiction.[105] This means that the Court of Appeal entertains appeals from civil cases tried by the High Court or by the subordinate courts. In the former category, the Court of Appeal would be the first level of appeal. In the latter category, it would be the second tier of appeal since the first would have been to the High Court.

Although the Court of Appeal is required to sit in panels of at least three or any greater uneven number of judges,[106] in practice, it

---

[102] S.C.J.A., s. 25.
[103] *Id.*, s. 28, and C.P.C., s. 268.
[104] S.C.J.A., s. 28 and C.P.C., s. 267(2).
[105] S.C.J.A., s. 29.
[106] *Id.*, s. 30.

invariably sits in panels of three. With only eight Supreme Court judges at present, and a heavy case-load, it is logistically not feasible to have panels of more than three judges hearing every appeal. Appeals are decided in accordance with the opinion of the majority of the judges on a panel.[107]

Section 34 of the Supreme Court of Judicature Act sets down the restrictions on the types of matters that may be brought before the Court of Appeal. For example, the amount in dispute at the trial must be at least $2,000. Otherwise, it is not appealable to the Court of Appeal except with the leave of that court or a Supreme Court judge.[108]

As with the High Court exercising appellate jurisdiction, appeals to the Court of Appeal are by way of rehearing.[109] In determining the appeal, the Court of Appeal may set aside or vary the judgment; confirm the judgment in whole or in part; remit the matter to the trial court to be retried; or make any other order(s) which the trial court could have made.[110]

c. *The Court of Criminal Appeal*

The Court of Criminal Appeal is the highest criminal court sitting in Singapore. It has jurisdiction to deal with two kinds of matters: first, appeals from decisions of the High Court exercising its original criminal jurisdiction;[111] secondly, points of law reserved arising in the course of a High Court trial[112] or in the course of an appeal from a subordinate court to the High Court.[113] There is no right of appeal to the Court of Criminal Appeal from a decision of a subordinate court in a criminal matter. Such a decision may only be appealed to the High Court exercising its appellate jurisdiction.[114]

However, a criminal case tried by a subordinate court may still

---

[107] *Id.*, s. 31.
[108] *Id.*, s. 34(1) (a), as amended by Act No. 4 of 1986.
[109] *Id.*, s. 37(1); Rules of the Supreme Court 1970 (hereinafter "R.S.C."), Ord. 57, r. 3(1).
[110] See S.C.J.A., ss. 37-40; R.S.C., Ord. 57, rr. 13-15.
[111] S.C.J.A., s. 44(1), as amended by Act No. 58 of 1973.
[112] S.C.J.A., s. 59(1).
[113] *Id.*, s. 60(1).
[114] See D. Marshall, "Appeals to Privy Council From Subordinate Criminal Courts in Singapore" [1969] 2 M.L.J. lxv; the exchange of correspondence between the Attorney-General and D. Marshall: [1970] 1 M.L.J. xiii, xxiv.

Legal Institutions 65

proceed to the Court of Criminal Appeal in the following way. Where the case has been appealed to the High Court exercising its appellate jurisdiction and the High Court has determined the appeal, the judge may, on the application of any party, reserve any question of law of public interest for the decision of the Court of Criminal Appeal.[115] If the application is by the accused, the judge has a discretion to refuse the application. However, where the application is by the Public Prosecutor, the judge must allow the application.[116] Questions of law of public interest include questions of law where there are conflicting judicial authorities.[117] In determining the question reserved, the Court of Criminal Appeal has the power to make such orders as the High Court might have made for a just disposal of the appeal.[118] Once a case has been heard by the Court of Criminal Appeal, it becomes possible to pursue it to the Privy Council since the Privy Council can only hear appeals from the Court of Appeal and the Court of Criminal Appeal.[119] From the foregoing, it may be seen that it is procedurally easier for the Public Prosecutor than for the accused to bring a criminal case tried by a subordinate court all the way to the Privy Council.

Criminal cases tried by the High Court may be appealed to the Court of Criminal Appeal. A convicted person may appeal against the conviction or the sentence or both.[120] The Public Prosecutor may appeal against the acquittal or the sentence.[121] In addition, having tried a criminal case, a High Court judge has the discretion to reserve any question of law arising in the course of the trial for the determination of the Court of Criminal Appeal.[122] However, where the Public Prosecutor is of the view that certain points of law should be considered by the Court of Criminal Appeal and certifies them accordingly, the High Court judge has no discretion to refuse, and thereupon, the Court of Criminal Appeal will consider the said points of law.[123] In determining the question(s) reserved, the Court of Criminal Appeal may alter the sentence passed and pass such sentence or

---

[115] S.C.J.A., s. 60(1).
[116] Id.
[117] S.C.J.A., s. 60(5) (a).
[118] Id., s. 60(4).
[119] See C.P.C., s. 241 and the Judicial Committee Act, Cap. 8, s. 2.
[120] S.C.J.A., s. 44(2).
[121] Id., s. 44(3).
[122] Id., s. 59(1) and C.P.C., s. 264(1).
[123] C.P.C., s. 264(3).

judgment or make such order as it thinks fit.[124]

As with its civil counterpart, the Court of Criminal Appeal usually sits in panels of three judges, which is the minimum number required by law.[125] Appeals are also decided in accordance with the opinion of the majority of the judges on a panel.[126]

In certain circumstances, the Court of Criminal Appeal has power to reject an appeal summarily without hearing it.[127] However, having heard an appeal, the Court of Criminal Appeal may exercise any power which the trial court might have exercised, and may confirm, reverse or vary the trial court's decision, or order a re-trial or remit the matter to the trial court with its opinion or order additional evidence to be taken or make any other order as it deems just.[128] The Court of Criminal Appeal is also empowered to dismiss an appeal if it feels that, notwithstanding its opinion that the point raised in the appeal might be decided in the appellant's favour, no substantial miscarriage of justice has occurred.[129] This ensures that a guilty person will not be acquitted on a mere technicality.[130]

3. The Subordinate Courts

A "subordinate court" is a court constituted under the Subordinate Courts Act and any other court, tribunal or judicial or quasi-judicial body from the decisions of which under any written law there is a right of appeal to the Supreme Court.[131] The major subordinate courts are the District Courts and the Magistrates' Courts. However, Juvenile Courts, Coroners' Courts and Small Claims Tribunals are also subordinate courts.[132] The President has power to constitute additional subordinate courts should the need arise.[133]

Subordinate courts are inferior courts. They only have limited

---

[124] S.C.J.A., s. 59(3).
[125] *Id.*, s. 43(1).
[126] *Id.*, s. 43(5).
[127] For example, where the grounds of appeal do not raise any question of law and the evidence is sufficient to support the conviction: see S.C.J.A., s. 52.
[128] S.C.J.A., s. 54 (as amended by Act No. 58 of 1973), s. 55.
[129] *Id.*, s. 54 (1).
[130] See e.g., the case of *Mimi Wong & Anor* v. *P.P.* [1972] 2 M.L.J. 75.
[131] See the definition of "subordinate court" in the S.C.J.A., s. 2.
[132] S.C.A., s. 3, as amended by the Small Claims Tribunals Act 1984, No. 27 of 1984, s. 45.
[133] S.C.A., s. 4.

Legal Institutions 67

original jurisdiction and are subject to the control and supervision of the Supreme Court. In March 1986, the civil jurisdiction of the District and Magistrates' Courts was increased five fold, and the criminal jurisdiction of the District Courts extended,[134] at the request of the judiciary.[135] This was done in order to reduce the workload of the High Court (which had increased by well over 100 percent over the preceding 5 years), and to minimise the time lag between the setting down of a case and its hearing in court.[136] This new arrangement is expected to reduce the High Court's civil case-load by about 60 percent.[137] To help the subordinate courts cope with their increased case-load, seven new judicial posts have been created.[138]

Unlike Supreme Court judges, subordinate court judges do not enjoy security of tenure. They are members of the Singapore Legal Service which is a public service.[139] As public servants, they hold office at the President's pleasure.[140] However, there is some constitutional protection for subordinate court judges in that public servants cannot be dismissed or reduced in rank without being given a reasonable opportunity to be heard.[141] Subordinate court judges also enjoy immunity from liability for acts done in the discharge of their judicial duty.[142]

a. *District Courts*

District Courts are presided over by District Judges appointed by the President on the recommendation of the Chief Justice.[143] A District Judge must have been a "qualified person" within the meaning of section 2 of the Legal Profession Act[144] for at least 5 years.[145] District judges are also *ex officio* magistrates.[146] On the recom-

---

[134] See the Subordinate Courts (Amendment) Act 1986, No. 3 of 1986, and the Criminal Procedure Code (Amendment) Act 1986, No. 5 of 1986, brought into force on 1 March 1986 by G.N. No. S 43/86 and No. S 41/86 respectively.
[135] See Singapore Parliamentary Debates Official Report, Vol. 46, cols. 698-699.
[136] *Id.*
[137] See *The Sunday Times*, March 2, 1986, p. 9.
[138] *Id.*
[139] Art. 102.
[140] Art. 104.
[141] Art. 110(3). See also, *infra*, Chapter IV.C.
[142] S.C.A., s. 68.
[143] *Id.* s. 9(1).
[144] Cap. 217. Reprint 1982. See *infra*, Chapter IV.B.1.(a), for an explanation of this term.
[145] S.C.A., s. 9(3).
[146] *Id.*, s. 9(5).

mendation of the Chief Justice, the President may appoint a Senior District Judge to oversee the administration of the subordinate courts.[147] A Senior District Judge has seniority over all other District judges.[148] One of his main responsibilities is to distribute judicial business in the subordinate courts.[149]

(i) Civil Jurisdiction

Generally, the District Court's civil jurisdiction is limited to $50,000.[150] Thus, disputes involving a higher amount necessarily have to go to the High Court unless the plaintiff is willing to limit his claim to $50,000,[151] or the action is founded on contract or tort and the parties agree to a District Court trial.[152] Similarly, the District Court has jurisdiction to try a dispute over title to land if the parties agree; but if any party disagrees, he may apply for the action to be transferred to the High Court.[153] The District Court also has a limited jurisdiction to grant probates and letters of administration for estates not exceeding $250,000.[154]

(ii) Criminal Jurisdiction

A District Court exercising criminal jurisdiction has the jurisdiction and powers conferred on it by the Criminal Procedure Code[155] and any other written law.[156] Generally, the criminal jurisdiction of the District Courts is limited to jurisdiction to try all offences punishable with fine only, or for which the maximum jail term does not exceed 10 years.[157] However, this general principle is subject to the following exceptions.

(1) The District Court may try cases other than those punishable with death provided the Public Prosecutor applies to the District Court to

---

[147] *Id.*, s. 9(2).
[148] *Id.*
[149] S.C.A., ss. 59-60.
[150] ss. 20-21, 25, S.C.A., as amended by Act No. 3 of 1986. The previous limit was $10,000.
[151] S.C.A., s. 22, as amended by Act No. 3 of 1986.
[152] *Id.*, s. 23, as amended by Act No. 3 of 1986.
[153] *Id.*, ss. 26-27.
[154] *Id.*, ss. 28-29, as amended by Act No. 3 of 1986. The previous limit was $50,000.
[155] Cap. 113, Reprint 1980.
[156] S.C.A., s. 50.
[157] C.P.C., s. 7(1), as amended by Act. No. 5 of 1986. The previous limit was 7 years.

Legal Institutions   69

try the offence and the accused consents to the application.[158]

(2) The District Court may try Penal Code offences shown in the eighth column of Schedule A of the Criminal Procedure Code to be triable by it.[159] Thus, the offence of committing robbery between sunset and sunrise[160] is triable by the District Court although it carries a maximum jail term of 14 years.

(3) Apart from Penal Code offences, offences under other laws may also be tried by the District Court where so provided by such laws.[161] For example, the Misuse of Drugs Act 1973[162] empowers the District Court to try offences thereunder although some of them carry a maximum jail term of 30 years or even the death penalty.[163]

The normal sentencing powers of the District Courts are spelt out in section 11(3) of the Criminal Procedure Code.[164] A District Court may pass any of the following sentences:

(a) a jail term not exceeding 7 years[165];

(b) a fine not exceeding $10,000[166];

(c) not more than 12 strokes of the cane;

(d) any combination of the above which it is legally authorised to impose;

(e) reformative training.

However, in the case of an accused with antecedents or previous convictions, the District Court's sentencing powers are enhanced. It may sentence the accused to a maximum jail term of 10 years, but must record its reason for doing so. The District Court may also have power to exceed its ordinary sentencing powers in section 11(5) where so authorised by other laws.[167] Thus, under the Misuse of Drugs Act 1973, except for the death penalty, District Courts have

---

[158] *Id.*, s. 7(2), as amended by Act No. 5 of 1986. Previously, District Courts had no power under the C.P.C. to try cases punishable with life imprisonment or death.
[159] *Id.*, s. 9(a).
[160] Penal Code, Cap. 103, s. 392.
[161] C.P.C., s. 9(b).
[162] Act No. 5 of 1973, Reprint 1978, s. 30.
[163] See *id.*, Second Schedule.
[164] As amended by Act No. 5 of 1986.
[165] The previous limit was 5 years.
[166] The previous limit was $5,000.
[167] C.P.C., s. 11(7).

the power to impose the full punishment prescribed by the Act (*i.e.*, a maximum of 30 years' imprisonment and 15 strokes of the cane).[168] It should further be noted that District Courts (and the High Court, but not Magistrates' Courts) may, in lieu of imprisonment, sentence repeat offenders to corrective training for 5 to 14 years or preventive detention for 7 to 20 years depending on their age and their record of previous convictions.[169]

b. *Magistrates' Courts*

On the recommendation of the Chief Justice, the President may appoint "any fit and proper person" to be a Magistrate.[170] However, a Magistrate must have been a "qualified person" (as defined in section 2 of the Legal Profession Act) for at least a year[171] before his appointment.

(i) Civil Jurisdiction

The civil jurisdiction of Magistrates' Courts is narrower than that of District Courts. It is limited to claims not exceeding $10,000.[172] Further, unlike District Courts, Magistrates' Courts have no jurisdiction in disputes over land title or to grant probates or letters of administration[173] at all.

(ii) Criminal Jurisdiction

A Magistrate's Court exercising criminal jurisdiction has the jurisdiction and powers conferred on it by the Criminal Procedure Code and any other written law.[174] In addition to trying criminal cases, magistrates perform a number of other duties. For example, they conduct preliminary inquiries with a view to committing a case for a High Court trial; they inquire into complaints of offences and issue warrants and summonses against offenders; they also issue search warrants and perform other functions which they are statutorily empowered to do.[175]

---

[168] s. 30, and Second Schedule.
[169] C.P.C., s. 12.
[170] S.C.A., s. 10(1).
[171] *Id.*, s. 10(2). For an explanation of this term, see *infra*, Chapter IV.B.1.(a).
[172] *Id.*, s. 52(1), as amended by Act No. 3 of 1986. The previous limit was $2,000.
[173] *Id.*
[174] S.C.A., s. 51.
[175] C.P.C., s. 8(1)(b)-(e).

Generally, the criminal jurisdiction of Magistrates' Courts is limited to trying offences punishable with fine only or offences for which the maximum jail term does not exceed 3 years.[176] However, as in the case of District Courts, this general rule is subject to several exceptions.

(1) Where an offence is triable by a District Court but not by a Magistrate's Court, the latter may nevertheless try the offence if the Public Prosecutor gives it written authorisation to do so.[177] Although such authorisation enhances the jurisdiction of the Magistrate's Court, it does not enlarge its normal sentencing powers.[178]

(2) Magistrates' Courts may try any Penal Code offence shown in the eighth column of Schedule A of the Criminal Procedure Code to be triable by them.[179] Thus, the offence of delivering a current coin with the knowledge that it is altered,[180] is triable by a Magistrate's Court although it carries a maximum jail term of 10 years.

(3) Apart from Penal Code offences, offences under other laws may also be tried by Magistrates' Courts where such laws so provide.[181] Thus, the Misuse of Drugs Act 1973[182] empowers Magistrates' Courts to hear and determine all proceedings under the Act although some offences under the Act carry a maximum punishment of 30 years' imprisonment, or even the death penalty. It should be noted, however, that although Magistrates' Courts have jurisdiction to hear and determine all proceedings under the Act, their sentencing powers are still circumscribed by the Criminal Procedure Code since the Misuse of Drugs Act[183] only enlarges the sentencing powers of District Courts but not those of Magistrates' Courts.

The normal sentencing powers of Magistrates' Courts are laid down in section 11(5) of the Criminal Procedure Code. A Magistrate's Court may pass any of the following sentences:

(a) a jail term not exceeding 2 years;

(b) a fine not exceeding $2,000;

---

[176] *Id.*, s. 8(1)(a).
[177] *Id.*, s. 10.
[178] *Id.*
[179] C.P.C., s. 9(a).
[180] Penal Code, Cap. 103, s. 251.
[181] C.P.C., s. 9(b).
[182] No. 5 of 1973. Reprint 1978, s. 30.
[183] *Id.*

(c) not more than 6 strokes of the cane;

(d) any combination of the above which it is legally authorised to impose.

However, in the case of a convicted person with previous convictions or antecedents, the Magistrate's Court has enhanced sentencing powers. It may impose the full punishment authorised by law even though this may exceed 2 years, but must record its reason for doing so.[184] The Magistrate's Court also has the power to exceed its ordinary sentencing powers where so authorised by other laws.[185]

c. *Coroners' Courts*

Coroners are appointed in the same manner as Magistrates. They must also possess the same qualifications.[186] In practice, Magistrates are concurrently appointed coroners as well.

The main responsibility of a coroner is to ascertain the cause and circumstances of death where there is reason to suspect that a person died in an unnatural manner *i.e.*, violently, suddenly or in an unknown way. He also ascertains whether any person was criminally involved in the cause of death.[187] The coroner performs these tasks by first making a preliminary investigation.[188] If the result of this exercise indicates that death was due to unnatural causes, the coroner will proceed to hold what is known as a coroner's inquiry or inquest.[189] Generally, a coroner will hold an inquiry in cases where the death was reported by the police. However, where the Public Prosecutor requests the coroner to hold an inquiry, the latter must do so.[190] To assist him in performing his functions, the coroner has power to order a *post mortem* examination of the body of the deceased.[191] He may also summon witnesses, and enjoys all the powers conferred on a Magistrate's Court in this connection as well as under Chapter XXXII of the Criminal Procedure Code.[192] After hearing the evidence, the coroner records his finding in writing.[193]

---

[184] C.P.C., s. 11(5).
[185] *Id.*, s. 11(7).
[186] S.C.A., s. 10.
[187] C.P.C., s. 283.
[188] *Id.*, s. 273.
[189] *Id.*, s. 275.
[190] *Id.*, s. 277.
[191] *Id.*, s. 281.
[192] *Id.*, s. 286.
[193] *Id.*, s. 290.

Legal Institutions

Since the responsibility of the coroner is limited to ascertaining the cause of death, any person revealed in the course of the inquiry as having caused the death of the deceased in a manner punishable under the Penal Code will be dealt with in separate proceedings.[194] However, if during an inquiry the coroner is informed that someone has been charged before a District Judge or Magistrate with causing the death of the deceased,[195] he must, unless there are reasons for doing otherwise, adjourn the inquiry till after the criminal proceedings conclude.[196] One reason for this practice may be to ensure that the inquest does not prejudice the trial of the person accused of causing the death of the deceased.[197]

d. *Juvenile Courts*

Compared to the subordinate courts mentioned above, Juvenile Courts are of more recent vintage. They were created by the Children and Young Persons Act 1949[198] for the express purpose of dealing with offences committed by children and young persons.[199] For the purposes of the Juvenile Court, a "child" is a person below the age of 14, and a "young person" is a person aged 14 or 15.[200] Thus, the juvenile courts deal with offences committed by young offenders below the age of 16.

However, it should be noted that the Juvenile Courts do not have exclusive jurisdiction over offences committed by such persons. A child or young person may still be tried by a court other than a Juvenile Court in three situations:

(1) where he is charged with an offence triable only by the High Court (*e.g.* murder), he will be tried by the High Court;

(2) where the child or young person is jointly charged with a person above 16, the charge will not be heard by a Juvenile Court but by a court of appropriate jurisdiction;

(3) where a person being tried by a court of appropriate jurisdiction

---

[194] *Id.*, s. 291.
[195] By murder, culpable homicide not amounting to murder, or a rash or negligent act.
[196] C.P.C., s. 279.
[197] See Myint Soe, *supra*, n. 7 at p. 88.
[198] Now known as the Children and Young Persons Act, Cap. 110, as amended by Act No. 21 of 1973, hereinafter "C.Y.P.A."
[199] *Id.*, s. 48.
[200] *Id.*, s. 42.

other than a Juvenile Court is, in the course of such proceedings, found to be a child or young person, that court may, nevertheless, if it thinks fit to do so, continue with the hearing and determine the proceedings.[201]

A Juvenile Court is presided over by a Magistrate nominated by the President.[202] He is assisted in his functions by two advisers who belong to a panel nominated by the President.[203] However, these advisers are not involved in the determination of the case. Their only function is to advise the Magistrate on considerations affecting the treatment of the child or young person brought before the court.[204]

The rationale behind the establishment of juvenile courts is clear. Young offenders are regarded as warranting a different approach and treatment from adult offenders.[205] Thus, they are dealt with by separate courts with special staff and procedures which indicate that, where young offenders are involved, the state's primary concern is their welfare.[206] Accordingly, the emphasis in the Juvenile Courts is on reform and rehabilitation rather than punishment.[207] Thus, for example, the Children and Young Persons Act contains provisions which ensure that a young offender is not treated as a criminal and is not made to regard himself as one before the court. Section 56 prohibits the use of the words "conviction" and "sentence" in relation to young offenders dealt with by a Juvenile Court. In their place, the words "a person found guilty of an offence, a finding of guilt or an order made upon such a finding", are to be employed. Juvenile court proceedings are also not open to the public. Only those directly concerned may attend.[208] In addition, the court is directed to use simple language in explaining the substance of the alleged offence to the young offender.[209] The philosophy behind the Juvenile Court is also seen in the orders it is empowered to make upon being satisfied that a child or young person has committed an offence.[210] The court may, *inter alia,* commit the offender to the care of a relative or other

---

[201] *Id.*, s. 48.
[202] *Id.*, s. 47(1).
[203] *Id.*
[204] C.Y.P.A., s. 47(3).
[205] *Id.*, s. 43(1).
[206] *Id.*
[207] *Id.*
[208] C.Y.P.A., s. 49(2).
[209] *Id.*, s. 57(1).
[210] *Id.*, s. 59.

Legal Institutions 75

fit person; or order his parent or guardian to execute a bond to exercise proper care and guardianship; or place the offender under probation for 1 to 3 years; or order the offender to be detained in a place of detention or remand home for not more than 6 months; or send the offender to an approved school for 3 to 5 years. The court may also order an offender to pay a fine, damages or costs, and has further powers to send a depraved or over-unruly offender to the Young Offenders Section of a prison. However, it has no power to order corporal punishment.

Appeals from Juvenile Courts lie to the High Court.[211]

e. *Small Claims Tribunals*

Small Claims Tribunals are the newest type of subordinate courts in Singapore. They only came into operation in early 1985[212] in response to the growing need "for a speedy and inexpensive machinery to handle small claims arising from disputes between consumers and suppliers"[213] and "to help consumers to protect themselves."[214] These tribunals also help to ease the case-load of the Magistrates' Courts.

The jurisdiction of Small Claims Tribunals is spelt out in section 5 of the Small Claims Tribunals Act 1984.[215] They only have jurisdiction to entertain disputes arising from contracts for the sale of goods or provision of services provided the claim does not exceed $2,000 and is brought within one year from the date on which the cause of action accrued.[216] Thus, the jurisdiction of a Small Claims Tribunal[217] is much narrower than that of a Magistrate's Court. It is limited to the resolution of small claims arising from defective goods or services. The government has explained that this is because these

---

[211] *Id.*, s. 61.
[212] The Small Claims Tribunals Act 1984, No. 27 of 1984, was brought into force on 15 January 1985 by G.N. No. S 18/85, dated 9 January 1985.
[213] Per Professor S. Jayakumar, the Minister for Labour and Second Minister for Law and Home Affairs, in moving the Bill at its second reading in Parliament: see Singapore Parliamentary Debates Official Report, Vol. 44, 24 August 1984, col. 1999.
[214] *Id.*, col. 2000.
[215] For a commentary on the Small Claims Tribunals Act 1984, see Ho Peng Kee, "Legislation Comments: The Small Claims Tribunals Act 1984" (1984) 26 Mal. L.R. 287.
[216] Small Claims Tribunals Act, No. 27 of 1984, (hereinafter "S.C.T.A."), s. 5.
[217] Hereinafter "Tribunal."

tribunals are at an experimental stage, and that their jurisdiction may be further extended if they prove successful.[218]

Each Tribunal is presided over by a Referee appointed by the President on the recommendation of the Chief Justice.[219] A Referee must be a "qualified person" within the meaning of the Legal Profession Act.[220] Referees hold office for such term as may be specified in the instrument of appointment, and may be reappointed from time to time.[221] However, their appointments may be revoked at any time by the President on the recommendation of the Chief Justice.[222]

The primary function of a Tribunal is to try to bring the parties to an agreed settlement.[223] In line with this basic philosophy, Tribunals are characterised by relatively flexible and informal procedure in sharp contrast to the other subordinate courts. Thus, lodging a claim is made a simplified task.[224] There is also an informal pre-hearing mediation attempt by the Registrar of the Tribunals,[225] which, if successful, results in an order giving effect to the terms of the settlement.[226] Such an order takes effect as an order of the Tribunal. Only when the pre-hearing settlement attempt fails will the hearing before the Referee take place.[227] Proceedings before the Tribunal are conducted in private[228] and in an informal manner.[229] Parties must present their own cases.[230] Except for corporate parties or the government which may be represented by an employee, no party may be represented whether by a lawyer or other agent, paid or otherwise.[231] In addition, the Tribunal is not bound by the rules of evidence but may inform itself on any matter in such manner as it thinks fit.[232] The Tribunal is authorised to control its own procedure,

---

[218] See *supra*, n. 213, at col. 2002.
[219] S.C.T.A., s. 4(1).
[220] *Id.*, s. 4(2).
[221] *Id.*, s. 4(3).
[222] *Id.*, s. 4(4).
[223] *Id.*, s. 12(1).
[224] *Id.*, ss. 15-16.
[225] *Id.*, s. 17(1).
[226] *Id.*, s. 17(2).
[227] *Id.*, s. 18.
[228] *Id.*, s. 22.
[229] *Id.*, s. 20.
[230] *Id.*, s. 21.
[231] *Id.*
[232] S.C.T.A., s. 25(1).

Legal Institutions

paying due regard to the principles of natural justice.[233] In determining the dispute, the Tribunal is directed to do so "according to the substantial merits and justice of the case," to have regard to the law but not to be bound to give effect to strict legal forms or technicalities.[234] In the light of the foregoing, it is not surprising that the Referee plays an active role in Tribunal proceedings and is more of a mediator than a judge. Nevertheless, proceedings before the Tribunal are judicial proceedings, at least where the privileges and immunities of Referees, parties, representatives and witnesses in the Tribunal proceedings are concerned.[235]

In determining a claim, the Tribunal has power to make several types of orders. It may dismiss the claim; or order one party to pay money to another party; or make a work (*i.e.* rectification) order against any party; or make a combination of the foregoing two orders.[236] The Referee's orders may be enforced using existing procedures available in the Magistrates' Courts.[237] Appeal from an order of the Tribunal lies to the High Court either on any ground involving a question of law, or on the ground that the claim fell outside the Tribunal's jurisdiction.[238]

4. The Shariah Court

A survey of the Singapore judicial system would be incomplete without mentioning the Shariah Court and its Appeal Board. As previously mentioned,[239] although the Singapore legal system is a predominantly common law one, there is a small degree of legal pluralism in that, in religious, matrimonial and related matters, the Muslim community is governed by a separate system of law administered by separate courts and judicial officers in accordance with the Administration of Muslim Law Act.[240]

In 1980, Muslims made up 16 percent of the population.[241] Rough-

---

[233] *Id.*, s. 27.
[234] *Id.*, s. 12(4).
[235] *Id.*, s. 41(2).
[236] *Id.*, s. 32.
[237] *Id.*, s. 33.
[238] *Id.*, s. 35.
[239] In Chapter I.D.
[240] Cap. 42, as amended by Acts no. 34 of 1973, No. 31 of 1975 and No. 31 of 1984, hereinafter "A.M.L.A."
[241] *Singapore Yearbook 1985*, p. 32.

ly 90 percent of the Muslims were Malays and the remaining 10 percent were of Indian and other non-Malay origin.[242] Thus, the system of law administered under the Administration of Muslim Law Act is generally Muslim law modified, where applicable, by Malay custom (*i.e. adat* law) specifically in matrimonial and related matters[243] and distribution of estates.[244] Malay custom would not apply to Muslims of non-Malay extraction. Since a significant percentage of Singapore society is governed by Muslim law, it is necessary to take a quick look at the courts which administer Muslim law in Singapore.

The Shariah Court and its Appeal Board were established by the Administration of Muslim Law Act.[245] The Shariah Court is presided over by a President appointed by the President of Singapore.[246] The jurisdiction of the Shariah Court is spelt out in section 35(2) of the Act. In order for the Shariah Court to have jurisdiction over a matter, two conditions must be satisfied. First, all the parties must either be Muslim or have been married under Muslim law. Secondly, the dispute must relate to marriage, divorce, betrothal, nullity of marriage, judicial separation, the disposition or division of property on divorce, or the payment of *mas kahwin*,[247] maintenance and consolatory gifts or *matta'ah*. As for procedure, the languages of the Shariah Court are Malay and English.[248] Further, the court is only to be guided by the principles of the law of evidence in Singapore and is not obliged to apply them strictly.[249] This is probably because the Shariah Court is essentially a family court, and therefore, flexibility in the proceedings is especially desirable. Appeal from a decision of the Shariah Court lies to an Appeal Board constituted under the Act.[250]

The Appeal Board is constituted by the President of the *Majlis Ugama Islam, Singapura*[251] from time to time, as the need arises.[252]

---

[242] *Id.*
[243] A.M.L.A., s. 35(3).
[244] *Id.*, s. 106.
[245] *Id.*, ss. 35 and 55 respectively.
[246] *Id.*, s. 35(1).
[247] *I.e.*, the obligatory marriage-payment due under Muslim law by the husband to the wife at the time the marriage is solemnized: see *id.*, s. 2.
[248] *Id.*, s. 37.
[249] *Id.*, s. 42.
[250] *Id.*, s. 55.
[251] *I.e.*, the Council of the Islamic Religion, Singapore.
[252] A.M.L.A., s. 55(4)-(5).

Legal Institutions

The *Majlis* advises the President of Singapore in matters relating to the Muslim religion in Singapore.[253] For example, on the advice of the *Majlis*, the President annually nominates at least 7 Muslims to form a panel from which the Appeal Board of 3 members is drawn. In entertaining an appeal from the Shariah Court, the Appeal Board has power to confirm, reverse or vary the decision of the Shariah Court or order a retrial. It can also exercise all the powers of the Shariah Court.[254] No further appeal lies from the decision of the Appeal Board.[255]

In addition to the Appeal Board, the Shariah Court is also subject to the control of the President of Singapore. The President has revisionary jurisdiction over the Shariah Court,[256] *i.e.*, he may call for the record of any proceedings before the court and may refer it to the *Majlis* for its consideration. The *Majlis* may recommend that the decision of the Shariah Court be reversed, altered or modified and the President may thereupon give effect to such recommendation by order.[257]

It may be noted that there is no overlap of jurisdiction between the courts created by the Administration of Muslim Law Act and the ordinary courts. The separateness of the respective jurisdictions of the Shariah Court and the ordinary courts is illustrated by the fact that even the High Court (which is the only court of general jurisdiction in the ordinary judicial system) has been statutorily deprived of jurisdiction to try any civil matters falling within the jurisdiction of the Shariah Court.[258] In addition, appeals from the Shariah Court lie only to the Appeal Board set up under the Administration of Muslim Law Act.[259] There is thus no contiguity between the Shariah Court and the ordinary courts, both in terms of jurisdiction and in terms of the systems of law they administer.

---

[253] *Id.*, s. 3.
[254] *Id.*, s. 55(6).
[255] *Id.*, s. 55(7).
[256] *Id.*, s. 56.
[257] *Id.*, s. 56(2).
[258] S.C.J.A., s. 16(1).
[259] A.M.L.A., ss. 55(1) and (7).

B. The Legal Profession [260]

The "legal profession" is a term commonly used to distinguish practising lawyers from other legally trained persons who do not practise law but instead work in banks, commercial firms, the Singapore Legal Service, government departments, *etcetera*. For the purposes of our present discussion, the term "legal profession" refers only to legal practitioners.

The Singapore legal profession dates back to the grant of the First Charter of Justice which set up a court for Penang.[261] As with many other Singapore legal institutions, the legal profession still retains characteristics which are traceable to its English ancestry. Nevertheless, differences between the English and Singapore legal professions do exist.[262] Most prominent of these is the fact that whilst the English legal profession has long been divided into two separate branches called barristers and solicitors, no such division exists in the Singapore legal profession, which is thus described as a "fused" one.

The Singapore legal profession has been fused from its inception.[263] This fusion had its genesis in the exigencies of early colonial conditions. The Charters had set up a system under which only law agents licensed by the Court could appear on behalf of suitors.[264] In those early days, however, no qualifications were stipulated for such agents,[265] probably because trained lawyers were in short supply. The first fully-qualified lawyer was admitted to the Singapore bar only in 1859.[266] It was not till 1873 that law agents were required to possess qualifications as British barristers or solicitors prior to admission to the Straits bar.[267] In 1878, the Courts Ordinance of the Straits Settlements gave statutory sanction to the position of "Advocates and Solicitors of the Supreme Court" as such by empowering the Supreme Court to admit British barristers and solicitors as Advocates

---

[260] See generally, Myint Soe, *supra*, n. 7 at pp. 92-107; "The Legal Profession" in the course materials for "Singapore Legal System" (Law/0/272/83), Faculty of Law, National University of Singapore, unpublished.
[261] Wee Chong Jin, "The Legal Profession in Singapore — Past, Present and Future" [1980] 2 M.L.J. lvii at lviii.
[262] See A.V. Winslow, "Some Reflections on Advocacy in a Fused Profession" (1973).
[263] *Supra*, n. 261.
[264] See Winslow, *supra*, n. 262 at p. 1.
[265] See C.M. Turnbull, *The Straits Settlements 1826-1867* (1972), p 71.
[266] *Id.*
[267] *Id.*, at p. 72.

and Solicitors of the Supreme Court, conferring that status on advocates and attorneys[268] already admitted in the Supreme Court before 1878, and giving Advocates and Solicitors of the Supreme Court the exclusive right to appear and plead in the courts.[269] From then onwards, and especially since 1907 when more comprehensive statutory provisions were made in this regard, statutory fusion of the two branches of the legal profession in Singapore became a *fait accompli*.[270]

In a similar fashion, the division of the legal profession into barristers and solicitors in England was more a product of historical accident than deliberate design.[271] Over the centuries, English barristers and solicitors came to divide up English legal practice between themselves. Generally, barristers specialise in advocacy (*i.e.*, litigation or presenting arguments in court) whereas solicitors specialise in general legal practice outside the realm of court work. Thus, solicitors do mostly paper work such as drafting wills, pleadings and other legal documents, as well as other work preparatory to court appearances (*e.g.* interviewing witnesses). Although solicitors may appear in county courts, they are not permitted to appear in the High Court and courts superior thereto. Only barristers may do so. Thus, in cases to be heard by the High Court, Court of Appeal or the House of Lords, solicitors must retain barristers. Although solicitors are permitted to deal directly with their lay-clients, barristers are not. A member of the public wanting to retain a barrister must do so in a somewhat circuitous fashion. He must first engage a solicitor who would then brief a barrister. The relative merits and demerits of fused or divided professions have been canvassed elsewhere and therefore will not be dealt with here.

In Singapore, every practising lawyer is an "Advocate and Solicitor of the Supreme Court" and therefore, in principle, entitled to do the work of both barristers and solicitors. In practice, however, many practitioners in the bigger firms tend to specialise in either solicitor's work *or* litigation. Some of the bigger firms even have litigation departments. Lawyers in these departments do most of the firm's litigious work although they may also do some solicitor's work from

---

[268] *I.e.*, solicitors.
[269] See Winslow, *supra*, n. 262.
[270] *Id.*
[271] See J.H. Baker, *An Introduction to English Legal History* (2nd ed. 1979), pp. 133-143.

time to time. However, the great majority of Singapore lawyers practise in small firms with only a few lawyers. In such firms, the lawyers usually do a mixture of solicitor's work and litigation.

In 1985, Singapore had approximately 1,200 private legal practitioners and roughly 100 government lawyers. This worked out to a ratio of about 1 lawyer per 2,000 head of population. A lawyer may practise alone, or in partnership with other lawyers, or as a legal assistant (*i.e.* "L.A.") in a law firm. The firm is owned by the partners, and the legal assistants are only salaried employees. Although there are a few big firms with more than a dozen partners, the great majority of law firms are quite small. In 1985, there were some 440 law firms. Apart from prudence and financial constraints, there is nothing to prevent a newly qualified legal practitioner from setting up his own law firm immediately.

The practice of law in Singapore is a monopoly reserved for advocates and solicitors of the Supreme Court. This principle is reflected in the Legal Profession Act[272] which gives advocates and solicitors the exclusive right to appear in court and makes it an offence for an "unauthorised person" to perform legal work.[273] In addition, an unauthorised person who undertakes legal work is specifically deprived of the fruits of his unlawful labour in that he is not allowed to sue for the costs of his services.

Since the legal profession enjoys a monopoly over the practice of law, it is necessary to ensure that certain standards of professional competence, conduct and ethics are maintained by the members of the profession. The question of competence will be dealt with first.

1. Maintaining Standards of Professional Competence

Minimum standards of professional competence are maintained by stringent control of entry into legal practice. In order to be entitled to practise law in Singapore, a person must become an Advocate and Solicitor of the Supreme Court, a process commonly known as being "called to the Bar." Generally, there are four categories of persons eligible to be admitted as advocates and solicitors. They are: qualified

---

[272] Legal Profession Act, (hereinafter "L.P.A."), Cap. 217, Reprint 1982, ss. 33-37.
[273] *Id.*, see s. 34(1) for the definition of "unauthorised person." There are exceptions to this rule: see *id.*, s. 36. For example, parties may act for themselves in a proceeding: *id.*, s. 36(1)(e).

persons, Malayan practitioners, Hong Kong practitioners and articled clerks.[274] These are the four main gateways into legal practice in Singapore. However, as will be apparent from the discussion that follows, each of these routes has its own requirements and some routes may be more difficult or narrower than others. Additionally, in particular cases, Queen's Counsel or other persons with special qualifications or experience for a particular case, are eligible to be admitted on an *ad hoc* basis.[275] Admission of persons to the Singapore Bar, whether generally or on an *ad hoc* basis, is not as of right, but lies at the discretion of the High Court.

The writer will now deal with the abovementioned four main routes into Singapore legal practice in greater detail.

(a) *Qualified Persons*

Paraphrasing section 2 of the Legal Profession Act,[276] the following are regarded as "qualified persons":

(i) local law graduates *i.e.*, holders of a Bachelor of Laws (i.e. LL.B.) degree from the National University of Singapore or its predecessors (namely, the University of Singapore and the University of Malaya in Singapore);

(ii) British barristers and solicitors;

(iii) holders of such other degree or qualification as may be recognised by the Minister of Law (on the advice of the Board of Legal Education) to be sufficient to qualify the holders thereof for admission to the Singapore Bar; such persons must also have obtained a certificate from the Board of Legal Education.[277]

At least 65 percent of practising lawyers in Singapore are local law graduates. Legal education in Singapore is essentially in the hands of two bodies: the Law Faculty of the National University of Singapore and the Board of Legal Education.[278] Academic legal education lead-

---

[274] *Id.*, s. 9, as amended by Act No. 17 of 1984, s. 4.
[275] L.P.A., s. 18.
[276] As amended by Act No. 17 of 1984, s. 2.
[277] L.P.A., s. 5A, inserted by Act No. 17 of 1984.
[278] The Board is made up of the Attorney-General, a Supreme Court judge nominated by the Chief Justice, two practitioners nominated by the Minister for Law, three practitioners nominated by the Law Society, the Dean of the Law Faculty of the National University of Singapore, and two members of the Faculty nominated by the Faculty: L.P.A., s. 6(1).

ing to the LL.B. degree (which makes the holders thereof "qualified persons") is left to the Law Faculty. Thereafter, it is the responsibility of the Board to provide for the training, education and examination of qualified persons intending to practise law in Singapore.[279] However, it is also one of the functions of the Board to make recommendations to the Law Faculty on matters involving the syllabi, course contents and examinations leading to the LL.B. degree.[280]

The third category of "qualified persons" was only added in August 1984.[281] The rationale behind expanding the pool of "qualified persons" and the consequent liberalization of entry into Singapore legal practice, was to enable talented lawyers from certain jurisdictions to practise in Singapore, and thereby inject the legal expertise necessary to stimulate Singapore's development as an international financial centre.[282] To date, law degrees from nine universities in Malaysia,[283] Hong Kong,[284] Australia,[285] New Zealand[286] and Canada[287] have been recognised by the Minister for Law (on the advice of the Board of Legal Education) as qualifying the holders thereof for admission to the Singapore Bar.[288] In making its recommendations, the Board selected "the more established university law degrees" which had "core curricula ... comparable with that of the Bachelor of Law (Honours) degree of the National University of Singapore."[289] It is anticipated that "[f]urther additions to the list of declared degrees will be considered from time to time in the light of experience and further investigations."[290]

---

[279] *Id.*, s. 4.
[280] *Id.*, s. 4(d).
[281] By Act No. 17 of 1984, s. 2.
[282] See generally, the speech of the Minister for Labour and Second Minister for Law and Home Affairs at the second reading of the Legal Profession (Amendment) Bill, Singapore Parliamentary Debates Official Report, Vol. 43, No. 17 at col. 1848.
[283] Bachelor of Laws (Honours), University of Malaya.
[284] Bachelor of Laws (Honours), University of Hong Kong.
[285] Bachelor of Laws (Honours) from the University of Sydney, the University of Melbourne and Monash University.
[286] Bachelor of Laws (Honours) from the University of Auckland and Victoria University of Wellington.
[287] Bachelor of Laws from the University of Toronto and Osgoode Hall, University of York.
[288] Pursuant to L.P.A., s. 5A(1). See G.N. No. S 51/85, No. S 56/85 and No. S 57/85.
[289] Press statement entitled "Recognition of Law Degrees From Foreign Universities" released by the Ministry of Law on 1 March 1985.
[290] *Id.*

There are additional requirements which "qualified persons" must satisfy before they can be admitted as advocates and solicitors.[291] They must be at least 21 years old and of good character. In addition, they must attend a 3-month postgraduate practical training course run by the Board of Legal Education, pass the examinations at the end thereof and then satisfactorily complete a 6-month pupillage period also known as "reading in chambers" or "chambering."[292] The postgraduate practical training course is a full-time course conducted by practitioners and is aimed at preparing law graduates for legal practice. Pupillage is essentially an apprenticeship to a lawyer of sufficiently senior standing in the profession in order to provide the aspiring practitioner with "on-the-job" training. During his pupillage, a "qualified person" is known as a "pupil" and the lawyer to whom he is apprenticed is known as his "master."[293] Upon completion of his pupillage, a pupil petitions the High Court to be admitted as an advocate and solicitor. If the High Court grants his petition (which it usually does as a matter of course), he is "called to the Bar" and his name is entered on the Roll of Advocates and Solicitors. Even then, he may not practise until he takes out a practising certificate.[294]

Generally speaking, all local law graduates (who make up the bulk of "qualified persons") must go through the 3-month postgraduate course and the 6 months of pupillage outlined above. However, the situation may be different for "qualified persons" who have relevant experience. Thus, where British barristers and solicitors or Commonwealth practitioners are concerned, the general postgraduate and pupillage requirements may be modified or waived at the Board's discretion[295] on a case-by-case basis. The same principle applies to Malayan and Hong Kong practitioners.[296]

(b) *Malayan Practitioners*

Malayan practitioners are another category of persons eligible to

---

[291] L.P.A., ss. 10-11.
[292] There is a possibility that the duration of the present postgraduate course and/or pupillage may be altered in the future.
[293] L.P.A., s. 11(1). To qualify to be a "master," an advocate and solicitor must have been in active practice in Singapore for at least 5 out of the 7 years immediately preceding his becoming a master: see *id.*, s. 12.
[294] *Id.*, s. 34(1).
[295] *Id.*, ss. 10(2) and 12(4).
[296] *Id.*, ss. 13, 13A and 12(4) (c).

enter Singapore legal practice. A Malayan practitioner is "any qualified person entitled to practise before a High Court in any part of West Malaysia."[297] *i.e.*, in addition to falling within one of the categories of "qualified persons" mentioned above, he must also have been called to the Malaysian Bar.

(c) Hong Kong Practitioners

In August 1984, Hong Kong practitioners became a new category of persons eligible for admission as advocates and solicitors. A Hong Kong practitioner is any person entitled to practise as a barrister or solicitor in Hong Kong.[298] However, to be eligible for admission into Singapore legal practice, a Hong Kong practitioner must have been actively practising as a barrister or solicitor in Hong Kong for a continuous period of at least 3 years prior to his petition for admission to the Singapore Bar.[299] He must also have obtained a certificate from the Board of Legal Education or the Attorney-General that, by reason of his qualifications and experience, he is a fit and proper person to be so admitted.[300] Even after he succeeds in gaining admission to the Singapore Bar, a Hong Kong practitioner is subject to certain restrictions in practising law in Singapore. As a general rule, he may only practise as a partner or associate or employee of an advocate and solicitor with at least 12 years' standing,[301] *i.e.*, he may not practise on his own initially. However, this restriction is lifted once the Hong Kong practitioner has practised in accordance with the said restriction for at least 2 years, and has, during that period, resided in Singapore for at least 12 months in the aggregate.[302] This practice restriction may also be completely waived by the Minister where he feels that a particular Hong Kong practitioner has sufficient standing and experience.[303]

The rationale behind opening the doors of Singapore legal practice to Hong Kong lawyers is probably, as one writer suggests, to attract talented Hong Kong lawyers troubled by the uncertain political fu-

---

[297] *Id.*, s. 2.
[298] *Id.*, s. 13A(6).
[299] *Id.*, s. 13A.
[300] *Id.*, s. 13A (2).
[301] *Id.*, s. 13A(4) (a).
[302] *Id.*, s. 13A(4) (b).
[303] *Id.*, s. 13A(5).

ture of Hong Kong, to emigrate to Singapore, bringing their skills and expertise with them.[304]

(d) *Articled Clerks*

Before the Legal Profession (Amendment) Act of 1984,[305] entering into articles of clerkship with an experienced solicitor was another way of gaining admission into legal practice. Articled clerks were similar to apprentices and learnt the ropes from their "principals." Articleship took at least five years and involved passing two sets of examinations covering a total of 15 subjects prescribed by the Board.[306] Articleship was an established route usually adopted by those who, for some reason or other, could not enrol in the LL.B. course in the Law Faculty as full-time law students. In the early years when there was no Law Faculty in Singapore, articleship provided a useful alternative for those who could not afford to study law in the U.K. However, the recent government view was that, with the establishment of the local Law Faculty in the late 1950s, articleship was no longer necessary.[307] In fact, they felt that articleship was being increasingly used as a backdoor into the legal profession by persons who would not have been able to make it to the Law Faculty on merit (*i.e.*, on the basis of their G.C.E. 'A' Level results).[308] Therefore, in 1984, articleship was abolished.[309] Thus, today, except for persons who were already articled clerks before the commencement of the Act, it is no longer possible to enter Singapore legal practice via articleship.[310]

To sum up, it may be seen that as a result of the Legal Profession (Amendment) Act of 1984, entry into Singapore legal practice has been liberalized by opening the doors to Hong Kong practitioners and a new category of "qualified persons." At the same time, it has been narrowed by the abolition of articleship.

---

[304] Soon Choo Hock, "Admission to the Legal Profession of Singapore — Opening 'Pandora's Box'?" [1985] 1 M.L.J. xxviii at xxxiv.
[305] No. 17 of 1984.
[306] This was the case for non-university graduate articled clerks: see the Legal Profession (Articled Clerks) Rules 1982, No. S 291/82, (as amended by No. S 193/84). rules 8-13. For graduate articled clerks, the requirements were laxer: see *id.*, rule 14.
[307] See Singapore Parliamentary Debates Official Report, Vol. 44, Second Reading of the Bill, at col. 1849.
[308] *Id.*, at col. 1854.
[309] Act No. 17 of 1984, s. 6.
[310] *Id.*, s. 9.

On the topic of legal practice in Singapore, it is germane to touch briefly upon the position of foreign lawyers in the Republic. Since 1980, the government has been allowing selected foreign law firms to set up branch offices in Singapore. Many of these are American, English and Australian firms engaged in "offshore work" *i.e.*, although physically located in Singapore, they do not do any work involving Singapore law, and confine themselves to international legal work, which is not seen as falling within the exclusive preserve of Singapore practitioners.[311] At present, there are some two dozen offshore firms and more than fifty offshore lawyers in Singapore. The basic rationale for allowing foreign law firms into Singapore is to help create the pool of international legal expertise necessary to build Singapore up as an international financial centre.

Many of the lawyers in these foreign firms are not qualified persons within the meaning of section 2 of the Legal Profession Act, or even if they are, are often not called to the Singapore Bar. As such, they are "unauthorised persons" within the meaning of section 34(1) of the Legal Profession Act, and are therefore not allowed to do legal work involving Singapore law. However, it should be noted that the line between work involving Singapore law and that involving foreign law is often difficult to draw, and this has been a source of growing concern among local practitioners who fear an increasing encroachment by foreign lawyers on their legal business in the long run.

The entry of foreign law firms and lawyers into Singapore is carefully controlled by the Attorney-General's Chambers in consultation with the Monetary Authority of Singapore and the Immigration Department.[312]

2. *Maintaining Standards of Professional Conduct and Ethics*[313]

In addition to being professionally qualified, legal practitioners are required to abide by certain standards of professional conduct and

---

[311] See generally, L.P.A., ss. 35-36.
[312] As with other foreign professionals, a foreign lawyer wanting to work in Singapore must first apply for an employment pass from the Immigration Department. The outcome of his application is likely to be strongly influenced by the views of the Attorney-General and the Monetary Authority of Singapore on the matter.
[313] See T.P.B. Menon, "Legal Profession in Singapore: Code of Ethics and Disciplinary Procedures" [1981] 2 M.L.J. v; M. Karthigesu, "Legal Professional Responsibility" in *Practice Law Manual: Vol. 1 — The Legal Profession* (R.J. Ennis ed.), pp. 123-149 (Board of Legal Education Practice Law Course, July 1985).

Legal Institutions 89

ethics. As a member of an honourable profession, a lawyer has a number of responsibilities.[314]

(a) His first duty is to the court. Under section 83 of the Legal Profession Act, every advocate and solicitor is an officer of the Supreme Court. This duty overrides his duties to all other persons, including his clients.

(b) A lawyer also owes a duty of his client. For example, he is expected to be professionally competent and to act in his client's best interests within lawful limits.

(c) A lawyer also has a duty to fellow members of the Bar *e.g.*, to honour undertakings to fellow practitioners and to be honourable and courteous in his dealings with them.

(d) A lawyer has a duty to the state. As with his duty to the court, this duty takes precedence over his duty to his client. Thus, for example, a lawyer must not assist his client in the commission of an offence.

The rules of conduct and practice governing advocates and solicitors are found in the Advocates and Solicitors (Practice & Etiquette) Rules,[315] the Legal Profession Act and various subsidiary legislation made pursuant to the rule-making powers under the Legal Profession Act.[316] These rules deal with various aspects of legal practice as well as professional etiquette and conduct. Thus, for instance, they stipulate conduct which is "unprofessional" or improper. For example, the Etiquette Rules specify that it is contrary to legal etiquette for an advocate and solicitor to solicit legal business[317] or advertise the address of his firm. It is also improper for an advocate and solicitor to share costs or profits with an unqualified person.[318]

The administration of the Singapore legal profession is primarily the responsibility of the Law Society of Singapore. All practising

---

[314] See R.J. Ennis, "Professional Responsibility" in *Practice Law Manual: Vol. 1 — The Legal Profession* (R.J. Ennis ed.), pp. 150-156 (Board of Legal Education Practice Law Course, July 1985).
[315] Hereinafter called the "Etiquette Rules," Gazette Notification No. 3137 of 1936, as amended in 1951, 1963, 1965, 1966 and 1970.
[316] E.g., The Solicitors' Accounts Rules 1985 (No. S 202/85), as amended by No. S 234/85 and No. S 326/85; The Solicitors' Trust Accounts Rules 1985 (No. S 203/85).
[317] *Supra*, n. 315, rule 5.
[318] *Id.*, rule 9.

lawyers are required by law to be members of the Law Society.[319] One of the more prominent purposes of the Law Society is to maintain and improve standards of professional conduct in the legal profession.[320] The primary way in which this purpose is carried out is through the Law Society's self-disciplinary mechanism. The Law Society takes upon itself the main responsibility of disciplining its errant members. The legal profession is the only profession in Singapore which regulates its own disciplinary procedure.[321]

Disciplinary proceedings may be initiated in two ways:

(1) where any person makes an application or complaint to the Law Society;[322] or

(2) where the Attorney-General or the Supreme Court or any judge thereof prefers information concerning the professional conduct of a lawyer to the Law Society.[323]

In the first situation, the Law Society Council (which is the executive body of the Law Society) will refer the matter to the Inquiry Committee which has the discretion to decide whether an inquiry should be held. In the second situation, however, the Inquiry Committee has no discretion and must hold an inquiry. The Inquiry Committee[324] is a body of 5 to 9 lawyers appointed by the Chief Justice to determine the facts and whether a matter should proceed to the Disciplinary Committee. The Disciplinary Committee[325] is an *ad hoc* committee of 3 to 5 practising lawyers appointed by the Chief Justice to hear and investigate any matter referred to it.

Upon completing its inquiry, the Inquiry Committee may recommend several possible courses of action to the Law Society Council. Where the matter is not serious enough, the Committee may recommend dismissal of the complaint or a penalty sufficient and appropriate to the misconduct committed.[326] If the Committee feels that the

---

[319] L.P.A., s. 42.
[320] *Id.*, s. 39(1) (a).
[321] See T.P.B. Menon, "Legal Profession in Singapore: Code of Ethics and Disciplinary Procedures" [1981] 2 M.L.J. v at x.
[322] L.P.A., s. 86(1).
[323] *Id.*, s. 86(2).
[324] *Id.*, s. 85.
[325] *Id.*, s. 91.
[326] In this regard, it may be noted that the Law Society has power to impose a fine not exceeding $5,000: see *id.*, ss. 88(1) (b) and 89.

matter is serious enough, it may recommend a formal investigation by the Disciplinary Committee. If a matter proceeds to the Disciplinary Committee, it may arrive at one of three possible determinations:[327]

(a) that there is no cause of sufficient gravity for disciplinary action under section 84 of the Legal Profession Act[328];

(b) that although there is no cause of sufficient gravity for disciplinary action under section 84, the lawyer in question should be reprimanded; or

(c) that cause of sufficient gravity for disciplinary action exists under section 84.

Section 84 gives the Supreme Court power to strike off the roll, suspend from practice or censure any advocate and solicitor on "due cause" being shown. The grounds for "due cause" are listed in section 84(2), the most commonly invoked being sub-clauses (2)(a) and (2)(b) *i.e.*, where the practitioner concerned has been convicted of a criminal offence, implying a defect of character making him unfit for his profession; or where he has been guilty of fraudulent or grossly improper conduct in the discharge of his professional duty or guilty of such breaches of any usage or rule of conduct made by the Law Society as are regarded by the court to be improper conduct or practice for an advocate and solicitor.

If the Disciplinary Committee recommends the third course of action mentioned above, the Law Society will apply to the High Court for an order calling upon the lawyer concerned to show cause why he should not be struck off the roll or suspended from practice or censured.[329] "Show cause" proceedings are heard by three Supreme Court judges including the Chief Justice.[330] Appeal from their decision lies directly to the Privy Council.[331] As in all criminal prosecutions, due cause in such "show cause" proceedings must be proved beyond all reasonable doubt.[332]

---

[327] *Id.*, s. 93(1).
[328] In this situation, it will not be necessary for the Law Society to take any further action in the matter unless so directed by the court: *id.*, s. 94(2).
[329] *Id.*, ss. 94(1) and 98.
[330] See *id.*, s. 98(6), and the definition of "court" and "judge" in s. 2.
[331] *Id.*, s. 98(6).
[332] See *Au Kong Weng v. Bar Committee, Pahang* [1980] 2 M.L.J. 89

In addition to disciplinary proceedings, a practitioner who breaches rules of professional conduct is quite likely to incur civil or criminal liability as well. Thus, misuse of client's money for example, may render a practitioner liable to criminal prosecution for criminal breach of trust[333] in addition to disciplinary proceedings. In this regard, it may be noted that where a practitioner has been convicted of criminal breach of trust or any other offence involving fraud and dishonesty, the matter will automatically go to a Disciplinary Committee for investigation as to whether or not the practitioner concerned should be disciplined.[334] Other breaches of professional conduct may attract civil liability in professional negligence in addition to disciplinary proceedings.

In summary, it may be said that the existence of the disciplinary mechanism as well as the possibility of encountering civil and/or criminal liability, are factors which help to ensure the maintenance of certain minimum standards of professional conduct and ethics among members of the Singapore legal profession. These devices safeguard the right of the public to legal services which are competently and ethically performed.

C. The Singapore Legal Service

During the colonial period, District Judges and most Magistrates were members of the Malayan Civil Service. There was no Legal Service Commission at that time and these legal officers were supervised by the Chief Justice and the Supreme Court.[335] However, in 1959, when the State of Singapore was created with internal self-rule, the new Constitution provided for the establishment of a separate Legal Service Commission[336] to supervise all officers in the public service who were required to have legal qualifications for their various appointments.

The Legal Service Commission thus established in 1959 continues to exist today on much the same basis. Its continued existence is provided for by Article 111 of the Constitution[337] and it is regarded as

---

[333] Under the Penal Code, Cap. 103, s. 409.
[334] See L.P.A., s. 86(5).
[335] See Myint Soe, *supra*, n. 7 at p. 107.
[336] Singapore (Constitution) Order in Council 1958 (1958) 2 U.K. S.I. 2156 (No. 1956).
[337] Reprint of the Constitution of the Republic of Singapore 1980.

Legal Institutions 93

part of the public service.[338] The Legal Service Commission is presided over by the Chief Justice. Its other members are the Attorney-General, the Chairman of the Public Service Commission, a Supreme Court judge nominated generally or specially by the Chief Justice, and not more than two members of the Public Service Commission nominated generally or specially by the Chairman of the Public Service Commission.[339] The Legal Service Commission has the responsibility of appointing, dismissing and exercising disciplinary control over officers in the Singapore Legal Service.[340]

Unless the Constitution expressly provides otherwise, Legal Service Officers, like other public servants, generally have no security of tenure but hold office at the President's pleasure.[341] However, as public servants, they are accorded some protection in that Article 110(3) provides that they cannot be dismissed or reduced in rank "without being given a reasonable opportunity of being heard." Also, according to Article 110(4), they cannot be "dismissed or reduced in rank by an authority subordinate to that which, at the time of dismissal or reduction, has power to appoint a member of that service of equal rank".

The Legal Service supplies legal officers to staff judicial positions in the courts[342] as well as legal positions in the many government departments, ministries and agencies.[343] The Legal Service has expanded in recent years because of an increasing number of trained lawyers being required to fill the above positions. For example, seven new judicial posts were recently created in the subordinate courts[344] to enable them to cope with the heavier caseload resulting from their newly extended jurisdiction.[345]

---

[338] Art. 102.
[339] Art. 111.
[340] *Id.*
[341] Art. 104.
[342] *E.g.*, Registrars, Deputy Registrars and Assistant Registrars of the Supreme and Subordinate Courts, Magistrates and District Judges.
[343] *E.g.*, Deputy Public Prosecutors in the Attorney-General's Chambers, Registrars and Assistant Registrars of Land Titles and Companies, Assistant Directors of the Legal Aid Bureau, etc.
[344] *The Sunday Times*, March 2, 1986, p. 9.
[345] The workload of the Subordinate Courts is expected to be more than doubled: *id.* For details on their recently increased jurisdiction, see *supra*, Chapter IV.A.3.

D. The Attorney-General[346]

The office of the Attorney-General of Singapore dates from 1867 when the Straits Settlements were made a Crown colony. This colonial legal institution has survived to the present. Article 35(1) of the Constitution establishes the office of the Attorney-General. The Attorney-General is appointed by the President on the advice of the Prime Minister, and he can only be appointed from among persons qualified for appointment as a judge of the Supreme Court. The Attorney-General is responsible to the Minister for Law, who is, in turn, responsible to Parliament for ensuring that the Attorney-General's Chambers are run in a satisfactory way.

According to the Constitution, the Attorney-General has two basic responsibilities. First, it is his duty "to advise the government on such legal matters and to perform such other duties of a legal character, as may from time to time be referred or assigned to him by the President or the Cabinet and to discharge the functions conferred on him by or under [the] Constitution or any other written law."[347] Secondly, he has sole discretion in deciding whether or not to institute, conduct or discontinue any proceedings under the criminal law[348] (*i.e.* sole prosecutorial discretion). In addition to these two constitutionally-founded responsibilities, it is an established principle of the common law that the Attorney-General is under a duty to protect the public interest. These then are the basic duties of the Attorney-General.

Since criminal prosecutions normally receive the most publicity, they are probably the most prominent part of the Attorney-General's functions in the eyes of the public. The Attorney-General is responsible for enforcing the criminal law on behalf of the State, and he performs this function in his capacity as Public Prosecutor.[349] In fulfilling this function, the Attorney-General has absolute prosecuto-

---

[346] See generally, Tan Boon Teik, "The Attorney-General" in a book of constitutional law essays to be published by the Malaya Law Review. The writer gratefully acknowledges the assistance of the Attorney-General in granting her permission to refer to this, as yet, unpublished work for the purposes of writing this section.
[347] Art. 35(7).
[348] Art. 35(8).
[349] For the role of the Public Prosecutor, see S. Rajendran, "Criminal Procedure in Singapore" in *Practice Law Manual: Vol 3 — Procedure* (R.J. Ennis ed.), pp. 828-832 (Board of Legal Education Practice Law Course, July 1985).

rial discretion and is assisted by members of his Chambers, *i.e.* Deputy Public Prosecutors.[350]

Although the Attorney-General is responsible for conducting criminal prosecutions, he is not directly involved in the investigations culminating in the prosecution. This is usually the province of the police, although they may seek the Attorney-General's advice on legal matters arising from such investigations. In the first instance, the police and other law enforcement agencies (such as the Central Narcotics Bureau) often have discretion in deciding whether or not a given matter should be referred to the Attorney-General's Chambers for prosecution. However, the final decision as to whether or not a matter should be prosecuted lies with the Attorney-General.

The civil aspect of the Attorney-General's functions receives far less publicity than the criminal aspect, but is no less important. The Attorney-General advises, and may represent the government or any of its agencies in any legal proceedings involving the latter. More generally, the Attorney-General also serves as legal adviser to the government and its agencies on various administrative and other matters.

The Attorney-General also wears another hat as guardian of the public interest. He is under a duty to protect and represent the public interest in cases where it is threatened. For example, he may intervene to prevent the misapplication of public funds, and to prevent government departments from abusing their authority.

To assist him in discharging his duties, the Attorney-General has a staff of legal officers which includes the Solicitor-General. The Attorney-General's Chambers have several divisions which reflect the various aspects of the Attorney-General's responsibilities. Thus, there is a criminal division (in charge of prosecutions), a civil division (which acts as legal adviser to the government), a legislative division (which is responsible for drafting all legislation and subordinate legislation) and a foreign affairs division (which deals with foreign and international relations *e.g.* keeping in touch with Law Reform Commissions in the Commonwealth, and giving legal advice to the Ministry of Foreign Affairs). There is also a securities division (which advises the Securities Industry Council) that was established as an

---

[350] C.P.C., s. 335(3). See J. Koh, "Criminal Law Practice in Singapore: The Prosecutor's Perspective" in *Practice Law Manual: Vol. 3 — Procedure* (R.J. Ennis ed.), pp. 810-811 (Board of Legal Education Practice Law Course, July 1985).

advisory and consultative body as well as to supervise takeovers and mergers, and approve all public share issues to be listed on the Stock Exchange. Lastly, there is a law revision division which is currently working on a new Revised Edition of the Laws of Singapore together with the Law Reform Commission of which the Attorney-General is the chairman.

E. Major Law Enforcement Agencies

Criminal and regulatory legislation are routinely enforced in the first instance by various government agencies such as the police, the Customs and Excise Department, the Commercial and Industrial Security Corporation, the Corrupt Practices Investigation Bureau or the Central Narcotics Bureau, as the case may be. In matters governed by such legislation, the citizen's first contact with the law is very likely to be with one of the major law enforcement agencies rather than with courts or lawyers. Lawyers and courts only enter the picture later, if at all. Thus, the major law enforcement agencies play a vital role alongside courts and lawyers in law enforcement and the administration of justice. An overview of Singapore's legal institutions would therefore be incomplete without briefly mentioning some of these agencies.

1. The Police Force

The police are the largest and oldest law enforcement agency in Singapore.[351] The primary functions of the Singapore Police Force are to maintain law and order, preserve the public peace, prevent and detect crimes and apprehend offenders.[352] Unlike other law enforcement agencies whose jurisdictions are much more specific and limited, the police can, in principle, investigate *any* offence. In practice, however, certain types of offences may be the prime responsibility of specialised law enforcement agencies. For example, drug offences and corruption are the specific responsibilities of the Central Narcotics Bureau and the Corrupt Practices Investigation Bureau respectively. Another basic difference between the police and other law enforcement agencies is the fact that only the police are charged with the general task of crime prevention.[353]

---

[351] The Singapore Police Force dates from 1821 when it began with a force of twelve men: see "Singapore Police Force — A Brief History" Police Life, May/June 1982, pp. 10-13.
[352] Police Force Act, Cap. 78, s. 8.
[353] C.P.C., s. 110.

The police constitute a vital component in the enforcement of law and the administration of criminal justice. They have the responsibility of making initial judgments on what conduct is criminal and of sufficient gravity to warrant setting the criminal justice process in motion. In performing their functions, the police work very closely with the Attorney-General's Chambers and with the courts. For instance, in criminal cases, the police are mainly responsible for the investigatory work, gathering facts and evidence, and apprehending, arresting or detaining offenders. In addition, every arrest must be reported to the Public Prosecutor.[354] The powers of police officers (*e.g.* to arrest, detain, search, *etcetera*) are set out primarily in the Criminal Procedure Code.[355]

When police investigations disclose an offence and identify the offender, it is ultimately up to the Attorney-General's Chambers to decide whether or not to initiate a criminal prosecution. Although the Attorney-General has sole prosecutorial discretion and is responsible for the conduct of all criminal prosecutions,[356] lesser crimes such as petty theft and traffic offences (which are essentially questions of fact and thus not expected to raise any questions of law) are routinely prosecuted by specially-trained police prosecutors who exercise limited prosecutorial powers[357] under the supervision of a Deputy Public Prosecutor. This arrangement eases the caseload of the prosecutors in the Attorney-General's Chambers.

In the interests of maintaining a higher standard of law and order, the Singapore Police Force has, in the last few years, made significant efforts to upgrade itself and to develop a closer rapport with the community.[358] Thus, programmes such as the Neighbourhood Watch Scheme (started in 1981), and the Neighbourhood Police Post System (inaugurated in 1983) and Crime Prevention Committees in commercial premises are designed to increase social awareness and community participation in crime prevention and detection.[359]

2. The Commercial and Industrial Security Corporation

The Commercial and Industrial Security Corporation is more

---

[354] *Id.*, s. 118(1).
[355] Cap. 113, Reprint 1980.
[356] Art. 35(8).
[357] See C.P.C., s. 335(8); J. Koh, *supra*, n. 350.
[358] See M. Cheang, "Changing Nature of Police Functions" [1985] 1 M.L.J. clxxviii at clxxxii.
[359] *Singapore Yearbook 1985*, pp. 204-205.

popularly known by the acronym "CISCO." It is a statutory board set up in 1972[360] to take over the functions of the former Guard and Escort Unit of the Singapore Police Force on a commercial basis.[361] The functions of CISCO are to provide guards and escorts for the protection of persons and property, to provide other security services and to co-operate as far as practicable and necessary with the Singapore Police Force in performing its functions.[362] Members, officers and employees of CISCO are deemed to be public servants within the meaning of the Penal Code.[363]

CISCO employees and officers may be authorised by the Commissioner of Police to carry such arms and accoutrements as may be necessary for the effectual discharge of their duties.[364] Every CISCO officer or employee so authorised to carry arms must be issued a warrant card by the Police Commissioner.[365] Until his warrant card is cancelled by the Commissioner, a CISCO officer or employee has the same powers and immunities as a police officer.[366] CISCO officers and employees may also be mobilised for active service by the Police Commissioner (with the approval of the Minister for Home Affairs) to perform either general or special police duties.[367] Whilst so mobilised, CISCO officers and employees have the same powers, duties, protection and immunities as police officers.[368]

3. The Central Narcotics Bureau

Singapore's position as a centre of international trade, shipping and communications, combined with its proximity to the infamous "Golden Triangle"[369] which supplies a significant portion of the world's heroin, have posed a lure to international drug syndicates and made it imperative for the Singapore government to combat the drug threat with stringent legislation and other means. The principal anti-

---

[360] By virtue of Act No. 18 of 1972.
[361] CISCO Annual Report 1982/83, p. 8.
[362] Commercial and Industrial Security Corporation Act 1972, No. 18 of 1972 (hereinafter "CISCO Act"), s. 7.
[363] *Id.*, s. 11.
[364] *Id.*, 12(1).
[365] *Id.*, s. 12(2).
[366] *Id.*, s. 12(3).
[367] *Id.*, s. 14.
[368] *Id.*, s. 14(3).
[369] An area straddling the borders of Burma, northern Thailand and Laos: see *The Sunday Times*, September 15, 1985, p. 9.

Legal Institutions 99

drug legislation is found in the Misuse of Drugs Act 1973, its subsequent amendments and subsidiary legislation made under the Act. The Central Narcotics Bureau[370] is the major government agency charged with drug enforcement in Singapore. In co-ordinating drug enforcement activities and gathering information relating thereto, the CNB works in close co-operation with the police and the Customs Department. On the international level, the CNB works closely with national drug enforcement agencies in many countries as well as with international agencies.

The Misuse of Drugs Act empowers the Director of the CNB to require any person he reasonably suspects to be a drug addict to be medically examined or observed by a government medical officer. If the result of the examination or observation is such that it is considered necessary for the person to be treated and/or rehabilitated at a Drug Rehabilitation Centre (*i.e.* DRC), the Director may order his admission to a DRC for treatment and/or rehabilitation for 6 months. Before the end of the 6-month period, a DRC Review Committee will review the case to determine whether the DRC inmate can be discharged from the DRC or transferred to the Day Release Scheme (*i.e.* DRS)[371] or detained for further treatment and rehabilitation. No person may be detained in the DRC for more than 3 years. Even after being discharged from the DRC, a person must undergo 2 years of supervision by the CNB's Supervision Division.

4. The Corrupt Practices Investigation Bureau[372]

Singapore has been relatively successful in containing the problem of corruption which is endemic in many developing countries. The CPIB has played no small role in this respect. It is the primary vehicle through which the Singapore government attempts to prevent and eradicate corruption in both the public and private sectors. The CPIB was set up in 1952 to take over the responsibility of the old Anti-Corruption Branch of the Singapore Police Force. It is a separate entity under the direct control of the Prime Minister. The CPIB derives its powers and existence from the Prevention of Corruption Act.[373]

---

[370] *I.e.*, CNB. See generally, *Singapore Yearbook 1985*, pp. 208-210.
[371] The DRS was set up in 1979 to assist treated drug addicts to reintegrate into society.
[372] Also known as the "CPIB". Some of the following information on this agency was drawn from a write-up kindly supplied by the Director of the CPIB on request.
[373] Cap. 104, as amended by Acts No. 27 of 1972 and No. 25 of 1981.

The Director and staff of the CPIB have wide powers to investigate corruption cases. For example, they have power to arrest without warrant, search arrested persons and take possession of articles believed to be evidence of corruption.[374] In addition, they may exercise the special powers which police officers possess when investigating seizable offences.[375]

In performing its functions, the CPIB works closely with the Attorney-General's Chambers. For instance, in certain situations, the powers of investigation of CPIB officers may be specifically enhanced by order of the Public Prosecutor.[376] Also, in cases where there is ample and concrete evidence of corruption, the matter is turned over to the Attorney-General's Chambers which has the final say on whether a criminal prosecution should be initiated.[377] In situations where the evidence of corruption is inadequate or weak, the matter may be referred to the Public Service Commission through the Permanent Secretary of the Ministry involved for suitable disciplinary action, which may result in a reprimand, a fine, a reduction in rank or dismissal from the service.

In addition to investigating corruption, the CPIB is also charged with the responsibility of preventing it. The CPIB has a special unit which has the function of researching the working procedures of corruption-prone departments to determine whether there are any administrative weaknesses which are conducive to corruption. If there are, the CPIB would make recommendations to the relevant head of department to eliminate such weaknesses.

5. *The Prisons Department*[378]

The Prisons Department manages eight penal institutions, five drug rehabilitation and three day-release centres. Its principal tasks are the safe custody and rehabilitation of convicted persons, detainees and drug abusers. The biggest penal institution is Changi Prison. Changi Prison and Queenstown Remand Prison are the two maximum security prisons which house persons convicted of more serious criminal offences, as well as criminal law detainees. There are

---

[374] *Id.*, s. 15.
[375] *Id.*, s. 16.
[376] See e.g., *id.*, ss. 17-18. They may also be specifically enhanced by a magistrate's warrant: *id.*, s. 21.
[377] See Prevention of Corruption Act, Cap. 104, s. 31.
[378] See generally, *Singapore Yearbook 1985*, pp. 211-212.

also three medium security prisons, a prison for female convicts, a Reformative Training Centre for young prisoners, and a minimum security prison (*i.e.* half-way house) for criminal law detainees on the day-release scheme. Of the five drug rehabilitation centres, four are for males and one is for females. These centres rehabilitate and treat drug addicts. The three day-release centres are half-way houses for drug addicts.

6. *The Customs and Excise Department*[379]

The Customs and Excise Department collects import and excise duties along with entertainments and film hire duties. The Department also acts as an agent for the Singapore Tourist Promotion Board in collecting the 3% cess from hotels, public houses and food establishments. In addition, the Department does agency work on behalf of other government departments and statutory organs by enforcing provisions of legislation such as the Misuse of Drugs Act, the Animals and Birds Act,[380] the Undesirable Publications Act,[381] the Control of Imports and Exports Act,[382] *etcetera*. This is a logical and expedient arrangement since all entry and exit points in Singapore are manned by Customs officers. In fact, Customs officers routinely help to prevent narcotic drugs and contraband from being smuggled into Singapore. Thus, they play an important role in the enforcement of certain laws.

---

[379] See generally, *id.*, pp. 129-130.
[380] Cap. 289.
[381] Cap. 107.
[382] Cap. 240.

Chapter V

Procedure

A. General

Like other common law systems, the Singapore legal system distinguishes sharply between civil and criminal proceedings because they serve very different purposes. The general objective of criminal proceedings is the punishment of offenders by the state. Any court proceeding which has a different objective may be loosely classified as a civil proceeding. Since crimes are wrongs committed against society, the state has a direct interest in bringing offenders to justice and thus assumes the role of the Public Prosecutor. Thus, criminal proceedings typically involve the state and private individuals. By contrast, civil actions typically involve disputes between private individuals over areas of private law such as tort, contract or property. The state has no direct interest in such actions, which merely provide private individuals with a forum for resolving their disputes. In most civil actions, the plaintiff's objective is to obtain a sum of money from the defendant, either as a debt, or as compensation for damage suffered by the plaintiff as a result of the defendant's wrongful act. Less frequently, a plaintiff in a civil action may seek other legal remedies such as specific performance, an injunction or a declaration.

Since criminal and civil proceedings have different objectives, it is understandable that they are governed by separate rules of practice and procedure. However, before we look at these rules in closer detail, it would be helpful to understand some of the fundamental assumptions on which they rest.

Many aspects of civil and criminal procedure in common law systems such as Singapore's have been shaped by the fact that jury trial was a cornerstone of English procedure for centuries. Although the jury system originated in the context of civil proceedings in England, it gradually became employed in criminal proceedings as well. By the time the British colonised Singapore in the nineteenth century, the jury had long become an established English legal institution with the function of deciding questions of fact.[1] Along with other English legal institutions and concepts, the jury system was

---

[1] Leaving questions of law to the judges.

adopted in Singapore for the trial of criminal matters only.[2] Jury trial was never adopted in civil cases. However, the jury was one English legal institution that exceptionally failed to take root in Singapore soil. It was found to be an ineffective device for administering criminal justice in Singapore.[3] Therefore, in 1960, jury trial was confined to capital offences, and in 1969, it was completely abolished.

With the exception of the United States, most common law systems that still retain the jury today no longer use it in civil cases. They use the jury only in criminal cases. The jury has fallen into decline in modern times because of various practical and administrative problems. Despite this, it is clear that the jury system has left lasting imprints on common law procedure. In fact, many aspects of procedure (especially civil procedure) in common law systems today have been shaped by the historical presence of the jury in the English common law system.[4] This observation is also true of the Singapore legal system although the jury system was abolished some fifteen years ago. The writer will now briefly highlight some fundamental features of Singapore civil procedure which are a legacy of the jury system.

As in other common law systems, a typical trial in Singapore is a single, "concentrated" event *i.e.*, at a preappointed time and place, the judge, the parties, their lawyers and witnesses are all convened in order to dispose of the matter once and for all. Concentration of trials is a practical and administrative necessity wherever juries are used. It is not possible to reconvene juries over an indefinite period since that would cause too much inconvenience and expense. Thus, the historical presence of the jury in the common law system led to the concentrated nature of common law trials. By contrast, the absence of the jury in civil proceedings in civil law systems meant that there was no need to concentrate the proceedings and therefore they tended to be

---

[2] Via the English Charters of Justice. For an interesting and amusing account of the operation of the jury system in the Straits Settlements from 1826 to 1867, see C.M. Turnbull, *The Straits Settlements 1826-1867* (1972), pp. 72, 134-137.

[3] See generally, M. Cheang, "Jury Trial: The Singapore Experience" (1973) 11 West Aust. L. Rev. 120; A.B.L. Phang, "Jury Trial in Singapore and Malaysia: The Unmaking of a Legal Institution" (1983) 25 Mal. L.R. 50. Among the reasons given by the government for abolishing the jury was the belief that the system enabled good, eloquent lawyers to get acquittals too easily, and that jurors were often ignorant and unreliable. See the comments of the Prime Minister in Parliament in 1959: Singapore Legislative Assembly Debates 1959, Vol. 2, col. 565.

[4] See J.H. Merryman, *The Civil Law Tradition* (2nd ed. 1985), pp. 111-123.

discontinuous. Thus, civilian trials tend to take the form of a series of conferences or hearings.

The concentration of common law trials in turn makes pre-trial proceedings very important. Since the case must be ready for trial and disposition in a single, concentrated event on the date(s) fixed, much preparatory work has to be done by the lawyers acting for each side. For example, the issues in dispute must be clearly and precisely defined for the court. In civil proceedings, this is the function of pleadings.[5] Questions of fact and law have to be carefully distinguished since the former are for the jury to decide whilst the latter are the judges' responsibility. Pleadings are therefore crucially important in preparing a civil matter for trial. Similarly, discovery and other pre-trial proceedings help the parties to ensure that the case is ready for trial and disposition on the date(s) set. By contrast, the discontinuous nature of civil proceedings in civilian systems means that pre-trial proceedings are correspondingly less important. Accordingly, their pleadings tend to be more general because the issues are expected to become more sharply defined in the course of the series of hearings. In fact, what we know as pre-trial proceedings in the common law system, tend, in the civil law system, to be merged with the trial itself. There is also no need to distinguish clearly between questions of law and fact in advance since the judge decides both and is capable of distinguishing them himself.

At the trial itself, concentration requires trial procedure to be tightly organised and well-structured.[6] However, this results in less flexibility in taking evidence. The element of surprise also becomes a real possibility because trial concentration may not allow the surprised advocate time to respond adequately. By contrast, the discontinuous nature of civil proceedings in civilian systems makes the hearings less structured and more informal, and also allows more flexibility in taking evidence. Witnesses may be called or recalled or further evidence introduced at any stage of the proceedings. This in turn reduces the element of surprise which is more likely to crop up in a common law trial.

The presence of the jury in the common law system also led to the

---

[5] This term refers to the Statement of Claim, the Defence, and further documents (if any) such as the Counterclaim, the Reply and the Rejoinder. See *infra*, Chapter V.C.1.a.

[6] *E.g.*, an opening address by the plaintiff's counsel, followed by the examination, cross-examination and re-examination of witnesses, *etc.*: see *infra*.

development of an elaborate and complex law of evidence. Most common law rules of evidence are exclusionary rules governing the admissibility of various types of evidence. An example is the hearsay rule. Such rules evolved from the historical need to protect layman (and in the early days, often illiterate) jurors from being misled by unreliable evidence. By contrast, the law of evidence in civilian systems is much less elaborate since no jury is involved.

Since the concentration of common law trials requires the lawyers on each side to do a great deal of preparatory work before the trial, it is not surprising that at the trial itself, the lawyers are in a much better position than the judge to dominate the proceedings. This has led to the common law trial being described as "adversarial" or "accusatorial" in nature, in contrast to the "inquisitorial" nature which is the hallmark of civilian trials. In adversarial systems, the judge characteristically plays a relatively passive role compared to the lawyers who typically take the lead in examining and questioning witnesses. The judge's job is to sit "to hear and determine the issues raised by the parties, not to conduct an investigation or examination on behalf of society at large ...."[7] The entire focus of the adversarial system is the trial itself which is essentially a contest between opposing counsel with the judge as a mere umpire.[8] By contrast, judges in inquisitorial systems play a much more active role in relation to the lawyers. An inquisitorial trial is in fact an inquiry into all the material circumstances of the case. It has been described as a collaboration to discover the truth. In this inquiry, the judge has general control over shaping and directing the proceedings, calling and examining witnesses and actively inquiring into the truth of the matter with the assistance of the lawyers on both sides. Unlike common law trials, there is no rigid procedure for examining witnesses,[9] and instead, witnesses are allowed to testify with fewer interruptions. All the information concerning the case goes into a *dossier*, which is a written record of each stage of the proceedings. While the actual trial is the focal point of the adversarial system, the *dossier* is the centrepiece of the inquisitorial system.

Another characteristic of common law procedure which may be attributed to the historical presence of the jury is "orality" *i.e.*, the

---

[7] *Jones v. National Coal Board* [1957] 2 All E.R. 155 at 159, per Lord Denning M.R.
[8] See David Marshall, "Facets of the Accusatorial and Inquisitorial Systems" [1979] 1 M.L.J. xxix at xxx, the Ninth Braddell Memorial Lecture, 1978.
[9] *I.e.*, the examination, cross-examination and re-examination of every witness: see *infra*.

oral presentation of all important aspects of the case before judge and jury.[10] Common law trials have traditionally emphasised orality. The historical reason behind this rule is the fact that, in the early days, many jurors were illiterate and therefore, to ensure that justice was not subverted, all evidence had to be orally presented before them. Thus, witnesses had to be sworn, orally examined and cross-examined in the presence of judge and jury. By contrast, civilian proceedings traditionally emphasised the *dossier* (*i.e.* the written record) as the result of medieval canon law influence.[11] In medieval canon law proceedings, evidence was normally taken by a clerk who had to reduce everything to writing. The judge based his decision on the clerk's written record. Although the modern civilian view recognises the importance of orality, the *dossier* remains the focal point in civilian proceedings.

It also remains a civilian practice to have the evidence taken, and the summary record prepared, by someone other than the judge who actually decides the case.[12] In civilian systems, all except the very lowest courts have collegial benches of three or more judges, only one of whom (normally the presiding judge) would follow the case from the beginning to the end in order to ensure some continuity in the proceedings. In deciding the case, the other judges who did not attend the entire proceedings would probably rely heavily on the *dossier* and the presiding judge. This "mediate" civilian practice contrasts sharply with the common law principle of "immediacy" which requires the evidence to be seen and heard firsthand by the judge who decides the case. There are rules of civil as well as criminal procedure in Singapore which reflect this emphasis on immediacy.[13] An insistence on orality makes immediacy an essential requirement. Conversely, for a mediate system to operate, it is essential to have written (rather than oral) proceedings.

From the foregoing, we can see that some of the fundamental assumptions underlying civil procedure in Singapore are concentration, an adversarial system, orality and immediacy. These principles are also generally applicable to criminal procedure. All these features were direct or indirect products of the jury system which was part of

---

[10] See *e.g.*, Rules of the Supreme Court 1970 (hereinafter "R.S.C."), Ord. 38, r. 1; The Subordinate Courts Rules 1986 (hereinafter "S.C.R."), Ord. 38, r. 1.
[11] See R.B. Schlesinger, *Comparative Law: Cases-Text-Materials* (4th ed. 1980), p. 392; J.H. Merryman, *The Civil Law Tradition* (2nd ed. 1985), pp. 113-114.
[12] See Merryman, *id.*; Schlesinger, *id.*, p. 407.
[13] See R.S.C., Ord. 35, r. 11; S.C.R., Ord. 35, r. 11; C.P.C., s. 199.

Singapore's common law heritage. Although the jury system became extinct in Singapore some fifteen years ago, many features of legal practice and procedure (*e.g.* an elaborate and complex law of evidence) which were shaped by the historical presence of the jury in England survive to the present day. The fact that many features of contemporary legal procedure in Singapore were shaped by an institution which no longer exists today may give pause for considering whether any of these features have outlived their usefulness and should therefore be discarded or modified so as to streamline Singapore legal procedure to better meet the needs of modern Singapore society. Such an inquiry, however, is beyond the scope of this work.

Nevertheless, it is hoped that the foregoing information will make the following examination of the details of Singapore civil and criminal procedure a little more meaningful.

B. Criminal Procedure[14]

Most systems of administration of criminal justice seek to balance two conflicting interests — society's interest in punishing the offender and deterring crime *versus* the need to protect the rights of the individual accused of committing an offence. This fundamental concern is seen in various aspects of criminal procedure. For example, one of the fundamental principles of Singapore criminal procedure is that the accused is presumed innocent until proven guilty. Another principle places the burden of proof on the Public Prosecutor to show that the accused is guilty of the offence charged. The Public Prosecutor must prove the accused's guilt beyond reasonable doubt. This is a higher standard of proof than in civil actions where a balance of probabilities is sufficient. The foregoing principles operate to protect the rights of the individual charged with committing an offence. Since a person convicted of an offence usually faces criminal sanctions which may range from monetary penalties or corporal punishment to loss of liberty or life, the above principles help to ensure that no person will be subjected to criminal sanctions unless his guilt has been proved to a high degree.

However, there are also features of the Singapore system of criminal justice which reflect society's interest in bringing offenders to

---

[14] See S. Rajendran, "Criminal Procedure in Singapore" in *Practice Law Manual: Vol. 3 — Procedure* (R.J. Ennis ed.), p. 812 (Board of Legal Education Practice Law Course, July 1985).

justice. For instance, in the last twenty years, criminal procedure has been amended to help the police and the prosecution to combat crime more effectively, and to deter crime. Accordingly, various measures have been adopted *e.g.*, abolishing the jury system and enhancing the punishments for various offences. Criminal procedure has also been tightened in order to enhance the chances of conviction of "determined criminals."[15] Towards this end, statements to the police have been made admissible and the right to silence of accused persons, during police investigations and in court, has been restricted.

The rules of general criminal procedure in Singapore are found primarily in the Criminal Procedure Code.[16] However rules of criminal procedure governing specific situations are also contained in a number of other statutes such as the Children and Young Persons Act,[17] the Criminal Justice (Temporary Provisions) Act,[18] the Preservation of the Peace Act,[19] the Misuse of Drugs Act,[20] the Internal Security Act[21] and the Criminal Law (Temporary Provisions) Act.[22]

Criminal procedure may be conveniently looked at in three phases: before, during and after the trial.

1. Pre-Trial Procedure

When the police receive first information concerning the commission of an offence, they file a "first information report."[23] This is where criminal prosecutions usually have their genesis. Receipt of such information triggers off police investigations, which make up the initial bulk of pre-trial procedure. However, not all complaints received by the police result in criminal prosecutions. In relatively minor matters (such as an assault in the context of a domestic quarrel), the police will normally not wish to take any action, and there-

---

[15] See the speech of the Minister for Law and the Environment at the second reading of the Criminal Procedure Code (Amendment) Bill in Parliament: Singapore Parliamentary Debates Official Report, Vol. 34, 19 August 1975, cols. 1217-1224.
[16] Cap. 113, Reprint 1980, as amended by Acts No. 10 of 1983, No. 9 of 1984, No. 24 of 1984, No. 5 of 1986, s. 3.
[17] Cap. 110, as amended by Act No. 21 of 1973.
[18] Cap. 111, as amended by Acts No. 21 of 1973 and No. 32 of 1975.
[19] Cap. 116.
[20] No. 5 of 1973, Reprint 1978; as amended by Act No. 28 of 1979.
[21] Cap. 115, as amended by Act No. 21 of 1973.
[22] Cap. 112, as amended by Acts No. 21 of 1973, No. 15 of 1974, No. 12 of 1976, No. 26 of 1979, No. 8 of 1981, No. 18 of 1984.
[23] C.P.C., ss. 114-116.

fore, if the complainant desires to pursue the matter, the police will refer him to a magistrate to file a private complaint and initiate a private prosecution. However, in more serious cases, the police will conduct further investigations, working closely with the Attorney-General's Chambers which ultimately decide whether to initiate a criminal prosecution.

The investigative powers of the police vary depending on whether "seizable" or "non-seizable" offences have been committed. "Seizable" offences are offences for which a police officer can ordinarily arrest without a warrant.[24] Generally speaking, these are the relatively more serious offences such as, for example, murder or housebreaking. Conversely, "non-seizable" offences are those which ordinarily require a warrant of arrest issued by a magistrate. In seizable offences, the police have wider powers of arrest, search and seizure than they do in non-seizable cases.[25] They also have power to compel the attendance of witnesses before them and to examine witnesses orally without first receiving authorisation from a Public Prosecutor or a Magistrate, which is the procedure in non-seizable cases.[26]

Just as the law arms the police with considerable investigative powers to assist them in protecting society's interest in crime detection and the punishment of offenders, it also lays down procedural safeguards to ensure that no person is deprived of his life or personal liberty "save in accordance with law." This fundamental right is enshrined in Article 9(1) of the Constitution.

Several legal rights emanate from this fundamental principle.

(a) An arrested person has a right to be informed, as soon as may be, of the grounds of his arrest.[27]

(b) He must also be allowed to consult and be defended by a legal practitioner of his choice.[28]

---

[24] *Id.*, s. 2: see the third column of Schedule A.
[25] *Id.*, ss. 115(2) and 117(1).
[26] See *id.*, and ss. 119-120, C.P.C.
[27] Art. 9(3).
[28] *Id.* See also, C.P.C., s. 194. However, this does not mean that there is a legal right to free legal aid for impecunious persons in criminal matters. At present, a somewhat paradoxical situation prevails in Singapore in that legal aid is legally available to impecunious persons in civil matters, but not in criminal matters. This is because Part II of the Legal Aid and Advice Act, Cap. 9, which was enacted 26 years ago and which provides for legal aid in criminal cases, has yet to be brought into force. For information on legal aid in Singapore, see K.S. Rajah, "Legal Aid in

(c) Where a person is arrested and not released, he must be produced before a magistrate without unreasonable delay, and in any case within 48 hours.[29]

(d) Where a person is being unlawfully detained, a complaint may be made to the High Court, whereupon the High Court will inquire into the complaint and order the release of the accused unless satisfied that his detention is lawful.[30] This is a procedure known as an application for *habeas corpus*.

In addition to the foregoing, the accused is presumed to be innocent pending the determination of his guilt at the trial. Thus, the law attempts to preserve the liberty of the accused during the pre-trial period through the mechanism of bail.[31] The bail system allows the accused to retain his personal liberty pending trial. At the same time, it ensures his attendance at the trial on pain of a pecuniary penalty to be exacted either from the accused himself or from his bailor, as the case may be. The bail system distinguishes between "bailable" and "non-bailable" offences.[32] Only persons to be tried for bailable offences have a right to bail, provided they are prepared to give bail.[33] In non-bailable offences, the accused has no right to bail, and the granting of bail is at the court's discretion.[34]

Singapore" in *Practice Law Manual: Vol 1 — The Legal Profession* (R.J. Ennis ed.), pp. 100-106 (Board of Legal Education Practice Law Course, July 1985). In capital offences, however, the High Court usually assigns counsel to such persons as a matter of practice: see Stanley Yeo Meng Heong, "Reopening the Case for Criminal Legal Aid in Singapore" [1983] 2 M.L.J. cxxiv at cxxviii. For other criminal offences, a destitute accused may seek the assistance of the Law Society or other private organisations of legal practitioners which offer free legal aid on a purely voluntary basis as a form of community service. With effect from 2 September 1985, the Law Society began a Criminal Legal Aid Scheme (CLAS) on a pilot basis. This scheme deals only with theft cases in its first year of operation but will eventually be extended to all criminal cases except some white-collar and capital offences. This scheme fills a significant gap in Singapore's legal aid facilities: see *The Sunday Times*, 1 September 1985, p. 20.

[29] Art. 9(4), as amended by Act No. 16 of 1984, s. 3.
[30] Art. 9(2).
[31] For more information on the bail system in Singapore, see S. Chandra Mohan, *Bail in Singapore* (1977).
[32] A "bailable offence" means an offence shown as bailable in Schedule A to the C.P.C. or which is made bailable by any other law for the time being in force, and "non-bailable offence" means any other offence: C.P.C., s. 2. Generally, offences punishable with a maximum of 3 years' imprisonment or with fine only are bailable.
[33] C.P.C., s. 350(1).
[34] *Id.*, s. 351.

Procedure 111

In many common law jurisdictions such as the U.K. and the U.S., an accused person also has a so-called "right to silence" which has traditionally been regarded as a procedural safeguard for the accused. In Singapore, however, the Criminal Procedure Code (Amendment) Act of 1976[35] has virtually extinguished the accused's so-called right to remain silent in the course of police investigations. This is an aspect of Singapore pre-trial criminal procedure which reflects society's interest in punishing and deterring criminals.

On being charged with an offence or being officially informed that he may be prosecuted for it, the accused is served a notice of warning which reads, in part, as follows:

> Do you wish to say anything in answer to the charge? If there is any fact on which you intend to rely in your defence in court, you are advised to mention it now. If you hold it back till you go to court, your evidence may be less likely to be believed and this may have a bad effect on your case in general.[36]

This "notice of warning" replaced the old "caution" which emphasised the right of the accused to remain silent. If the accused remained silent at the time he was charged, the court has a discretion to draw adverse inferences against him at the trial.[37]

There is yet another aspect of pre-trial criminal procedure in Singapore which reflects the public interest in punishing and deterring criminals. In the course of police investigations, important statements are often made to the police by the accused. Previously, with a few exceptions, such statements were generally inadmissible in evidence. However, since the 1976 Amendment Act, this position has changed radically. Today, any statement made at any time by the accused to a police officer of at least the rank of sergeant is admissible in evidence provided the statement was made without threat or inducement *i.e.* voluntarily.[38]

Once the police complete their investigations and the Public Prosecutor decides to initiate a criminal prosecution, the case will be prepared for trial. The charge(s) will be drafted and read out at a magistrate's or other court, which will also fix the trial date. Depen-

---

[35] No. 10 of 1976.
[36] C.P.C., s. 121(6).
[37] *Id.*, s. 122.
[38] *Id.*, s. 121(5).

ding on the gravity of the offence, the accused may be tried in a Magistrate's Court, a District Court or the High Court.

2. Trial Procedure

Criminal trial procedure in the subordinate courts is slightly different from that in the High Court. A High Court trial is normally preceded by a preliminary inquiry conducted by a magistrate, the aim of which is to determine whether there are sufficient grounds for committing the accused to a High Court trial.[39] At this stage, the prosecution need only show sufficient evidence against the accused. It is not necessary to prove his guilt beyond reasonable doubt until the trial itself. By contrast, cases to be tried by Magistrates' Courts or District Courts do not require preliminary inquiries but are tried summarily, and are therefore referred to as "summary trials." Although the High Court generally does not try criminal matters that have not first undergone a preliminary inquiry, it may do so in certain circumstances *e.g.*, where the High Court transfers a case pending in a subordinate court to itself.[40]

As a general principle, all criminal cases are tried by a single judge sitting alone.[41] The only exception to this rule is the trial of capital offences, which must be conducted by a court consisting of two High Court judges.[42]

a. *Summary Trials*

As explained above, trials in the subordinate courts are normally conducted summarily. The procedure for such trials is set out by sections 179 and 180 of the Criminal Procedure Code. The main steps may be summarised as follows.

(i) The accused is brought before the court.

(ii) The charge is then read and explained to him and he is asked whether he pleads guilty or not guilty.

(iii) The accused then pleads guilty or not guilty. If he keeps quiet, his silence has the same effect as a plea of not guilty.

---

[39] *Id.*, ss. 141-142.
[40] See *id.*, s. 184, and the case of *T.T. Rajah* v. *R.* [1963] M.L.J. 281.
[41] See *e.g.*, S.C.J.A., s. 10.
[42] C.P.C., s. 193(1).

(iv) If the accused pleads guilty:

(a) the court must, before it records that plea, ascertain that the accused understands the nature and consequences of the plea and intends to admit the charge without qualification;

(b) the prosecution then reads out the statement of facts;

(c) the accused admits the facts stated;

(d) the court accepts the accused's guilty plea and convicts him;

(e) a plea of mitigation may then be made on behalf of the accused;

(f) the sentence is passed, and the trial is concluded.

Thus, in cases where the accused pleads guilty, the trial proceedings are shortened and simplified.

(v) If the accused pleads not guilty, a normal full-length trial is set in motion, and the court proceeds to hear the complainant (if any).

(vi) However, before the court examines the complainant, the accused may request for an amendment of the charge. The charge may then be amended if the prosecution consents.

(vii) The prosecution may then open its case and call its witnesses. It is not necessarily the case that the court will examine the complainant first. In fact, for reasons of convenience, it is often the practice to examine certain non-controversial witnesses[43] before the complainant. Throughout the trial, it is the general duty of the prosecution to prove its case beyond reasonable doubt.

(viii) After the prosecution examines its witnesses, the accused has the right to cross-examine them. The prosecution then has the right to re-examine those witnesses.

(ix) At the conclusion of the prosecution case, the accused may submit that there is "no case to answer" *i.e.*, that the prosecution has failed to prove its case.

(x) Where the accused makes such a submission, arguments by both sides would then be presented.

(xi) At this point, the court must decide whether the prosecution has made out a case against the accused "which, if unrebutted, would

---

[43] Who, as a matter of policy or convenience, should not be kept waiting for too long *e.g.* doctors giving medical evidence.

warrant his conviction."[44] At this stage, the prosecution must have made out a *prima facie* case.[45] If it has not, the court will acquit the accused. If it has, the court will call upon the accused to enter upon his defence.

(xii) At this stage, the court will consider whether the charge requires any amendment. If the charge is amended, it must be read and explained to the accused once more, and he must again be asked whether he is guilty or has any defence to make. Charges can be amended at any time before judgment is given.[46] In practice, however, the charge is usually amended early in the trial rather than midway through it.

(xiii) Before the court calls upon the accused to present his defence, the court must, in ordinary language, warn the accused of the consequences that might follow if he refuses to be sworn or affirmed. Since 1976,[47] an accused person has only two options in a trial. If he wants to give evidence, he must do so under oath or affirmation.[48] The alternative is to remain silent. The first option renders the accused liable to cross-examination.[49] The second allows the court, in ascertaining his guilt, to draw such inferences from the silence as appear proper.[50] However, this does not mean that the accused can be compelled to give evidence on his own behalf.[51]

(xiv) The accused (or his lawyer) may then open his case. If the accused chooses to give evidence, his evidence will be taken before that of other defence witnesses.

(xv) The defence witnesses will then be examined, cross-examined and re-examined.

---

[44] C.P.C., s. 179(f).
[45] See *Haw Tua Tau* v. *P.P.* [1981] 2 M.L.J. 49, Privy Council.
[46] C.P.C., s. 162.
[47] Before 1976, an accused person had the additional right of making an unsworn statement from the dock, on which he could not be cross-examined. Since such a statement could not be tested by cross-examination, it had little probative value. In 1976, this right of the accused was abolished. This move was part of the overall policy to curtail the accused's right to silence both before and during the trial since it was felt that this so-called "right to silence" often operated to hamper the administration of criminal justice *i.e.*, it had the effect of protecting the guilty.
[48] C.P.C., s. 195(1).
[49] *Id.*
[50] C.P.C., s. 195(2). However, adverse inferences will not be drawn if the accused has lawful reasons for remaining silent *e.g.*, privilege: *id.*, s. 195(4).
[51] He is not liable for contempt of court if he remains silent or refuses to be sworn or affirmed: *id.*, s. 195(3).

(xvi) At any time while he is making his defence, the accused has the right to recall and cross-examine any witness present in the court or its precincts.

(xvii) At the conclusion of the defence, the accused (or his lawyer) may sum up his case.

(xviii) If he does so, the prosecution will have a right to reply.

(xix) The court then decides whether the accused is guilty. If it finds him not guilty, it will order an acquittal.

(xx) If the court finds the accused guilty, he (or his lawyer) will be given the opportunity to make a mitigation plea before the court pronounces the sentence.

(xxi) The court then records a conviction and passes sentence on the accused.

b. *High Court Trials*

Apart from capital offences, which must be tried before two judges, all trials in the High Court are conducted by one judge.[52] How did capital offences come to have a different mode of trial? For the ten years preceding the complete abolition of the jury system in 1969, jury trials were retained only in capital offence cases. Then, when the jury system was finally totally abolished in 1969, an appropriate replacement had to be found for the trial of capital offences. The "two-judge" trial system was decided upon as a suitable substitute.[53] In such a trial, the accused can only be sentenced to death if both judges unanimously find him guilty of the capital offence.[54] If they are not unanimous, then he may, if the two judges agree, be convicted of a lesser offence.[55] In the event of disagreement between the two judges during the trial concerning matters of procedure or admission or rejection of evidence, the presiding judge has the casting vote.[56]

The procedure for High Court trials is outlined in sections 186 to 195 of the Criminal Procedure Code. It is much the same as trial procedure in the subordinate courts. The only significant differences

---
[52] See S.C.J.A., s. 10, read with C.P.C., s. 193.
[53] One of the two judges would be the presiding judge: C.P.C., s. 193(1).
[54] *Id.*, s. 193(2).
[55] *Id.*, s. 193(3).
[56] *Id.*, s. 193(4).

are that whilst the prosecution's opening speech is optional at a summary trial,[57] it is compulsory at a High Court trial;[58] also, unlike the position in summary trials,[59] the prosecution in a High Court trial has the right to reply on the whole case regardless of whether the accused produces evidence or not.[60]

Once the court finds the accused guilty, it will proceed to convict and sentence him. The punishment for each offence is prescribed by law. Punishments for criminal offences range from the death penalty, which is reserved for the most serious offences (*e.g.* murder and certain arms or drug offences) to life imprisonment, imprisonment for shorter terms, corporal punishment, preventive detention, corrective training, fines or probation, depending on the gravity of the offence.

3. Post-Trial Procedure

Once the court has pronounced judgment, the trial is ended. Thereafter, the party dissatisfied with the court's decision may file a notice of appeal.[61] The procedure for appeals from the subordinate courts to the High Court is outlined below. Except where mentioned in the footnotes, appeals from High Court trials follow much the same procedure.

The accused may appeal against the judgment, sentence or order on the ground that there is an error of law or fact[62]; and/or he may appeal against the sentence on the ground that it was manifestly excessive.[63] However, an accused person who pleads guilty and is convicted on that plea may only appeal against the sentence, but not against the conviction.[64] The prosecution, on the other hand, may appeal against the accused's acquittal or against the sentence on the ground that it was manifestly inadequate.[65] The notice of appeal must

---

[57] *Id.*, s. 180(a).
[58] *Id.*, s. 187(1).
[59] *Id.*, s. 180(c).
[60] *Id.*, s. 190.
[61] *Id.*, s. 246(1).
[62] *Id.* Appeals from High Court trials may be on questions of law or fact or mixed fact and law: S.C.J.A., s. 44(4).
[63] C.P.C., s. 246(1).
[64] *Id.;* S.C.J.A., s. 44(2), as amended by Act No. 58 of 1973.
[65] C.P.C., ss. 244 and 246(1); S.C.J.A., s. 44(3).

be filed within 10 days from the date of the judgment.[66] A major reason for the brevity of this period is probably to discourage frivolous appeals.

Once the notice of appeal has been lodged, the court appealed from has to furnish the appellant with the grounds of decision[67] so that the latter may be able to formulate his grounds of appeal. However, the Criminal Procedure Code is conspicuously silent as to when the court must do this.[68] Although the Code does not specify a time limit, cases have said, and rightly so, that the grounds of decision should be sent to the appellant without too much delay.[69] In any case, once the appellant receives the grounds of decision, he has 10 days within which to file his petition of appeal.[70] The petition must set out the grounds of appeal. The procedure at the hearing is laid down in section 252 of the Criminal Procedure Code.

Although the Criminal Procedure Code prescribes the procedure and deadlines which appellants from Subordinate and High Court trials must satisfy, it also gives the appellate courts power and discretion to allow an appeal notwithstanding the non-observance of any formal requirements.[71] This is to ensure that substantial justice will be done in the matter.

A pending appeal generally does not have the automatic effect of staying execution of the judgment.[72] The only exceptions to this general principle are where the accused has been sentenced to corporal punishment or death.[73] In these two situations, the sentence

---

[66] C.P.C., s. 246(1). For appeals from the High Court to the Court of Criminal Appeal, the time limit is 14 days: S.C.J.A., s. 45(1).
[67] C.P.C., s. 246(3). However, in the case of an appeal from a High Court trial, the appellant has to take the initiative to procure a copy of the record of the proceedings from the High Court Registry for a prescribed fee: S.C.J.A., s. 46. The grounds of decision or written judgment are part of the record of the proceedings.
[68] C.P.C., s. 246(3); S.C.J.A., s. 46(1), as amended by Act No. 58 of 1973.
[69] See *Nathan v. P.P.* [1978] 1 M.L.J. 134; *P.P. v. Woon Chin Fatt* [1948-9] M.L.J. 131. In the case of an appeal from a High Court trial, s. 46(2) of the S.C.J.A. requires the Registrar to serve a notice on the appellant to inform him of the availability of the record of proceedings "as soon as possible after notice of appeal has been filed." This suggests that the trial judge is correspondingly expected to produce a written judgment (containing the grounds of decision) without too much delay.
[70] C.P.C., s. 246(4); S.C.J.A., s. 47(1).
[71] C.P.C., s. 249; S.C.J.A., s. 50.
[72] C.P.C., s. 250; S.C.J.A., s. 51.
[73] C.P.C., s. 227; S.C.J.A., s. 51.

will not be carried out until the deadline for filing a notice of appeal has expired, or, where a notice of appeal has been filed, until the appeal has been determined. In all other situations, the trial or appellate courts have the discretion to stay execution on any judgment, order, conviction or sentence pending appeal on such terms as to security for the payment of any money, or the performance or non-performance of any act or the suffering of any punishment ordered, as to the court seem reasonable.[74] Apart from a stay of execution, a convicted appellant may also apply for bail pending appeal.[75] However, the considerations in such a case are different from an application for bail pending trial because there is no longer a presumption of innocence (since the accused has been found guilty) and there is also an increased risk of the accused absconding from the jurisdiction because of the sentence imposed. Therefore, generally, the graver the offence and the heavier the sentence appealed from, the more difficult it is for a convicted appellant to obtain bail pending appeal.

A person convicted in a subordinate court trial only has the right to appeal to the High Court.[76] He has no right to appeal further to the Court of Criminal Appeal. However, he may apply to the High Court to reserve a question of law of public interest for the decision of the Court of Criminal Appeal.[77] From the Court of Criminal Appeal, it is possible for either party to pursue an appeal to the Privy Council provided special leave is granted by the latter.[78] By contrast, a person convicted in a High Court trial has the right to appeal to the Court of Criminal Appeal.[79] If special leave is granted, he may pursue the matter to the Privy Council.[80]

---

[74] *Supra*, n. 72.
[75] C.P.C., ss. 247, 250 and 353.
[76] For details on the powers of the High Court exercising appellate criminal jurisdiction, see *supra*, Chapter IV.2.a. (iv).
[77] See *supra*, Chapter IV.A.2.c.
[78] See *supra*, Chapter IV.A.1.
[79] For details on the powers of the Court of Criminal Appeal, see *supra*, Chapter IV.A.2.c.
[80] For further details on appeals, revision, *etc.*, see Chapter IV.A.: The Judicial System.

Procedure 119

C. Civil Procedure[81]

Because litigation is often expensive and time-consuming, it is usually the least favoured method of settling a dispute. In fact, a high proportion of civil disputes is settled out of court through less formal mechanisms such as arbitration, mediation or negotiation. This commonly occurs even where legal proceedings have already been initiated. Litigation is typically resorted to only when informal settlement attempts have failed.

Civil litigation is regulated by rules of civil procedure which all who invoke the civil process must observe.[82] Apart from certain types of proceedings such as bankruptcy and winding-up proceedings which are regulated by separate sets of rules,[83] general civil proceedings in the Supreme Court are governed by the Rules of the Supreme Court 1970[84] and those in the subordinate courts by the Subordinate Court Rules 1986.[85] These rules of procedure were not enacted by Parliament but are subsidiary legislation drafted by committees comprising mainly judges and some legal practitioners.[86] The rules of civil procedure in Singapore courts are very similar to those applicable in English courts because Singapore borrowed very heavily from England in this area. In fact, the 1970 Supreme Court rules are substantially based on the English Rules of the Supreme Court, Revision 1965. They are almost identical except for some modifications in the former to suit local circumstances. The Rules of the Supreme Court 1970 is divided into sections called "orders" which are in turn further sub-divided into "rules."

Before he can start an action in court, the plaintiff must determine a number of preliminary matters such as the cause of action (*i.e.* the

---

[81] See "An Introduction to Civil Court Procedure" in *Practice Law Manual: Vol. 3 — Procedure* (R.J. Ennis ed.), pp. 549-563 (Board of Legal Education Practice Law Course, July 1985); Myint Soe, *The General Principles of English Law* (Rev. ed. 1982), pp. 112-120; Chang Min Tat, *Mallal's Supreme Court Practice: Vol. 1* (2nd ed. 1983).
[82] See R.S.C., Ord. 1, r. 2(1); S.C.R. Ord. 1, r. 2(3).
[83] See R.S.C. Ord 1, r. 2.
[84] Made by the Supreme Court "Rules Committee" pursuant to the powers conferred by s. 80 of the S.C.J.A.
[85] Made by the Subordinate Courts "Rules Committee" pursuant to s. 69 of the S.C.A.
[86] See S.C.J.A., s. 80(3); S.C.A., s. 69(4); R.S.C., pp. 5 and 475; S.C.R., pp. 104 and 569.

legal theory on which his claim against the defendant is founded), the parties (*i.e.* who he wishes to sue) and the court in which he should commence his action. The appropriate court is usually determined by the amount claimed or the value of the subject matter in dispute. For example, if the plaintiff's claim is below $10,000, he should sue in a Magistrate's Court.[87] Once he has determined the foregoing matters, the plaintiff may proceed to commence his action in court.

Since civil procedure in the subordinate courts closely follows that in the High Court,[88] we will take a look at High Court civil procedure first.

1. Civil Procedure in the High Court

As with criminal procedure, civil procedure may be conveniently looked at in three phases: before, during and after the trial.

a. *Pre-Trial Procedure*

There are four ways of commencing an action in the High Court, *i.e.*, by writ of summons,[89] originating summons, originating motion or petition. The plaintiff must determine the appropriate mode to use because the court has a discretion to set aside, in part, the proceedings commenced by the wrong mode.[90] The R.S.C. sets out the circumstances in which each particular mode is to be employed.[91] For example, proceedings may only be begun by originating motion or petition where expressly stipulated by law.[92] Further, an action may be commenced by originating summons only where the key issue is one of the construction of legislation or a written document or some other question of law, or where there is unlikely to be any substantial dispute of fact.[93] Generally, the most common way of commencing a High Court action is by writ.

The writ is taken out by the plaintiff against the defendant. It is a

---

[87] For more details on the civil jurisdiction of Singapore courts, see *supra*, Chapter IV.A: The Judicial System.
[88] See the new Subordinate Courts Rules 1986, and *infra*.
[89] Hereinafter "writ."
[90] R.S.C., Ord. 2, r. 1. Unless otherwise indicated, all references to "Ord." and/or "r./rr." hereinafter are to the R.S.C.
[91] Ord. 5.
[92] For example, the Divorce Procedure Rules stipulate that all actions for divorce must be commenced by petition.
[93] Ord. 5, r. 4(2).

Procedure 121

command to the defendant by the President of the Republic to enter an appearance within 8 days[94] if he desires to dispute the plaintiff's claim. The writ must be indorsed either with a Statement of Claim or a concise statement of the nature of the plaintiff's claim or the remedy sought so as to inform the defendant of the nature of the plaintiff's claim against him.[95] To ensure that the defendant has notice of the writ, the law generally requires a copy of the writ to be personally served on the defendant.[96] Where personal service is not possible because the defendant cannot, for some reason, be located, the court may allow such substitutes for personal service as to the court seem just (e.g. service by post or advertisement).[97] Where the defendant is abroad, a notice of the writ may be served outside the jurisdiction.[98]

Once the writ has been served upon the defendant, he has 8 days within which to enter an appearance if he intends to defend the action against him.[99] The defendant enters an appearance by handing in or posting a memorandum of appearance and a copy thereof to the Supreme Court Registry.[100] The memorandum is a request to the Registrar to enter appearance for the defendant.[101] The copy is then sent to the plaintiff so that the latter is notified that the defendant has entered an appearance.[102] If the defendant fails to enter an appearance, he is assumed to admit the plaintiff's claim, and the plaintiff may then proceed to apply to the court for a judgment against the defendant in default of appearance.[103]

However, if the defendant enters an appearance, the next important step is the exchange of pleadings.[104] Pleadings are formal documents containing concise statements of the material facts[105] relied upon by the party pleading. The basic pleadings in most cases are the plaintiff's Statement of Claim and the defendants' Defence (and

---

[94] See Ord. 6, r. 1 and Form 2, R.S.C.
[95] Ord. 6, r. 2(1).
[96] Ord. 10, r. 1.
[97] Ord. 62, r. 5.
[98] See Ord. 11.
[99] Ord. 12, r. 4(a).
[100] Ord. 12, r. 1(3).
[101] Form 15, R.S.C.
[102] Ord. 12, r. 3.
[103] Ord. 13.
[104] See Ord. 18.
[105] Ord. 18, r. 7(1).

Counterclaim, if any). Less commonly, there may be further pleadings such as the plaintiff's Reply and the defendant's Rejoinder. In practice, however, most pleadings rarely go beyond the Reply stage.

Pleadings serve two main purposes.[106] First, they identify the issues in dispute to the court in advance so that the court may expeditiously resolve the dispute at the trial. Secondly, pleadings also give the other party fair notice of the case to be met so that he will not be taken by surprise at the trial. For these two reasons, parties are bound by their pleadings, *i.e.*, they may not raise at the trial matters which were not pleaded.[107] Thus, pleadings have to be very carefully drafted. However, there are provisions for the amendment of pleadings in appropriate circumstances.[108]

At any time before the pleadings are closed, a party may, without leave of the court, deliver interrogatories relating to any matter in dispute to the other party.[109] Interrogatories are written questions requiring the party interrogated to answer upon oath.[110]

Fourteen days after the service of the Defence (or the Reply as the case may be), the pleadings are deemed to be closed[111] so that the issues to be decided by the court are as identified in the pleadings.

Once the plaintiff has served his Statement of Claim on the defendant and the latter has entered an appearance, the plaintiff may apply for summary judgment on the ground that the defendant has no defence to the action.[112] This procedure prevents a defendant who has no real defence from taking advantage of the judicial process to prolong litigation and delay judgment for the plaintiff. Applications for summary judgment are normally heard by the Registrar in chambers. If the defendant wants to defeat the plaintiff's application for summary judgment, he must convince the Registrar that there is a "triable issue"[113] *i.e.*, that there is an issue or question which ought to be tried. If the Registrar believes that there is no *bona fide* defence, he will give judgment for the plaintiff. However, if he feels

---

[106] See D.B. Casson and I.H. Dennis, *Odgers' Principles of Pleading and Practice in Civil Actions in the High Court of Justice* (22nd ed. 1981), pp. 87-88.
[107] See *Waghorn v. George Wimpey & Co. Ltd.* [1970] 1 All E.R. 474.
[108] Ord. 20.
[109] Ord. 26, r. 2.
[110] See Forms 49 and 50, R.S.C.
[111] Ord. 18, r. 20.
[112] Ord. 14, r. 1.
[113] Ord. 14, r. 3(1).

that there is a triable issue, the plaintiff's application for summary judgment will be dismissed and the matter will proceed to trial. Just as the plaintiff may apply for summary judgment to avoid protracted litigation where there is no real defence, so the defendant is similarly able to apply to the court to strike out the plaintiff's Statement of Claim where it reveals no reasonable cause of action.[114]

Once the pleadings have closed and the issues have been identified, the next step is the discovery and inspection of documents.[115] This procedure enables each party to have notice of his opponent's documentary evidence. The parties are required by law to exchange lists of documents which are or have been in their possession, custody or power relating to the matters in question in the action.[116] This must be done within 14 days of the close of pleadings.[117]

The last stage in pre-trial procedure is when the plaintiff takes out a summons for directions.[118] This has to be done within one month of the close of pleadings.[119] The purpose of this step is to allow the court to thoroughly take stock of the issues to be tried and the manner in which evidence should be presented at the trial in order to shorten the length of the trial and to save costs generally. Thus, at the hearing of the summons, all matters which must or can be dealt with by interlocutory applications but have not already been so dealt with, will be dealt with as far as possible.[120] Once this is done, the court will give directions regarding the future conduct of the action, including the trial itself. For example, the court may fix the period within which the plaintiff must apply to the Registrar to set the action down for trial.

b. *Trial Procedure*[121]

At the trial, it is the responsibility of the plaintiff to convince the court that he has a legal right to a remedy. He must prove each and every element of his cause of action on a balance of probabilities. The standard of proof in a civil action is thus lower than that in a criminal

---

[114] Ord. 18, r. 19.
[115] See Ord. 24.
[116] Ord. 24, rr. 1-2.
[117] Ord. 24, r. 2(1).
[118] Ord. 25.
[119] Ord. 25, r. 1(1).
[120] *Id.*
[121] See Ords. 35, 38-39.

action. Be that as it may, the general rule applicable to both types of action is that, a party alleging any fact must prove it[122] unless the law of evidence presumes its existence.[123]

Where the defendant is concerned, he is not required to disprove the plaintiff's claim. He need only show, by cross-examination of the plaintiff's witnesses for example, that the plaintiff has not proved his case on a balance of probabilities. However, if the defendant admits the facts alleged by the plaintiff but wants to rely on new facts, he must prove them.

The trial usually begins with an opening speech by the plaintiff's counsel.[124] This is meant to give the trial judge an overview of the main facts and issues in dispute. The plaintiff's counsel then proceeds to call his witnesses. This is called "examination-in-chief." The defendant then has the right to "cross-examine" the plaintiff's witnesses, after which the plaintiff may "re-examine" them.

At the end of the plaintiff's case, the defendant must decide whether he wants to adduce evidence. If he chooses not to do so, the plaintiff will make a closing speech and the defendant must then state his case. However, if the defendant decides to adduce evidence, his counsel may make an opening speech and then call the defence witnesses. The witnesses are examined following the same procedure used for the plaintiff's witnesses. At the end of the defendant's case, his counsel will make a closing submission following which the plaintiff will have the right of reply.

It should also be noted that at the end of the plaintiff's case, the defendant has the right to make a submission of "no case to answer" where the plaintiff has failed to adduce at least *prima facie* evidence against the defendant.[125] In practice, however, the making of such a submission in a civil trial is rarely done because the defendant must be prepared to stand or fall on that submission alone. This is because the trial judge will normally refuse to rule on the submission unless the defendant agrees to call no evidence if his submission is rejected.[126] The rationale behind this judicial practice is as follows:

---

[122] Evidence Act, Cap. 5, s. 101.
[123] See e.g., *id.*, ss. 113-114.
[124] Ord..35, r. 4(2).
[125] See Casson and Dennis, *supra*, n. 106 at pp. 298-300.
[126] See *Payne* v. *Harrison & Anor* [1961] 2 Q.B. 403; *Parry* v. *Aluminium Corpn.* [1940] W.N. 44.

(a) it is highly inconvenient to require the judge, as judge of fact, to express any opinion on the evidence until he has heard all of it; (b) if the judge rules in favour of the submission and that ruling is reversed on appeal, the matter would go back to trial and the witnesses who were not heard would be called again to give evidence; unnecessary expense and inconvenience would thereby be caused.[127]

At the end of the trial, the judge delivers his decision. Judgment must be pronounced in open court either immediately after the trial or on a subsequent date of which due notice has been given to the parties.[128]

The usual remedy sought by plaintiffs and granted by courts in civil actions is damages. This is a lump sum assessed by the court as the loss suffered by the plaintiff as a result of the defendant's conduct. Other remedies which a court may award in civil proceedings include equitable remedies such as injunctions and orders of specific performance. An injunction is a court order prohibiting the doing of a particular act. By contrast, an order of specific performance compels the performance of a particular act. However, equitable remedies are a matter of judicial discretion. For a variety of reasons, they are awarded much less often than damages. For example, the courts will generally refuse to award specific performance where damages are adequate.[129]

a. *Post-Trial Procedure*

(1) Enforcement of Judgment

Even after the trial has ended and judgment has been delivered, a successful plaintiff may have to take further steps in order to enjoy the fruits of his victory. The judgment by itself operates as a declaration of the respective rights and liabilities of the parties. There is no problem if the judgment debtor[130] willingly complies with the judgment by paying the assessed damages, interest and costs to the judgment creditor.[131] However, if he refuses or is unable to do so, the judgment creditor must take steps to enforce the judgment. The

---

[127] See *Alexander* v. *Rayson* (1936) 1 K.B. 169 at 178 (Court of Appeal).
[128] Ord. 42, r. 1.
[129] See e.g., *Ryan* v. *Mutual Tontine Westminster Chambers Association* [1893] 1 Ch. 116 at 126, per Kay L.J.
[130] As the defendant is known once judgment has been awarded in favour of the plaintiff.
[131] *I.e.*, the successful plaintiff.

law provides a variety of devices to assist him in doing so.[132] For example, the judgment creditor may apply to the court for a writ of *fieri facias* which commands the sheriff to seize and sell such of the debtor's goods as is necessary to discharge his own costs as well as the judgment debt and costs. Alternatively, where a third party owes a sum of money to the judgment debtor, the judgment creditor may apply for a garnishee order requiring the third party to pay the debt directly to him. A judgment for the payment of money may also be enforced by way of a charging order or the appointment of a receiver. In cases where the court has ordered an injunction or specific performance, non-compliance constitutes a contempt of court which is punishable with committal to prison.[133] Needless to say, the threat of imprisonment is a strong inducement to compliance with a court order.

(2) Appeals

A dissatisfied party in a High Court civil trial has a right to appeal to the Court of Appeal. The detailed rules governing this appellate civil procedure are found in the Supreme Court of Judicature Act[134] and the Rules of the Supreme Court.[135] The main steps in this procedure may be outlined as follows.

The appellant is required to file a notice of appeal within one month of judgment.[136] The notice of appeal must clearly and concisely indicate the parts of the judgment to be appealed against.[137] Copies of the notice of appeal must then be served on all parties directly affected by the appeal.[138]

Once the notice of appeal is filed, the trial judge is required to certify in writing the grounds of his judgment or order unless he had already delivered a written judgment.[139] The Registrar then informs the appellant as soon as possible that the record of the proceedings is available.[140] Within one month therefrom, the appellant is required

---

[132] Ord. 45.
[133] Ord. 45, r. 5.
[134] ss. 29-41.
[135] Ord. 57.
[136] *Id.*, r. 4.
[137] *Id.*, r. 3(2).
[138] *Id.*, r. 3(6).
[139] *Id.*, r. 5(1).
[140] *Id.*, r. 5(2).

Procedure 127

to file his petition of appeal, which must clearly and concisely state the grounds of appeal.[141] Within 10 days of filing the petition of appeal, the appellant must file 4 copies of the record of appeal and serve a copy on every respondent.[142] After that, the appeal will be listed for hearing.

At the hearing, counsel for the appellant will submit his arguments first. After that, the respondent's counsel will reply. In hearing the appeal, the Court of Appeal has the same powers as the trial court.[143] In fact, the appeal is by way of a re-hearing[144] and, therefore, the appellant may challenge the judgment on both facts as well as law. However, appealing on questions of fact is not commonly done, and the Court of Appeal will only admit fresh or additional evidence on "special grounds."[145] An appeal to the Court of Appeal generally does not have the automatic effect of staying execution of the judgment appealed against.[146]

A party dissatisfied with the judgment of the Court of Appeal may appeal still further to the Privy Council,[147] provided leave from the Court of Appeal is first obtained.[148] However, litigants rarely pursue a matter to the Privy Council. One of the main reasons is the prohibitive cost of doing so. In fact, as mentioned earlier, litigation is often expensive and time-consuming. The longer the duration of a proceeding and the higher the tribunal, the greater the expenses incurred. Thus, a general objective of civil procedure is to reach a just settlement of the dispute whilst at the same time trying to shorten proceedings and save costs as far as possible.[149] Evidence of this philosophy is seen in the fact that the rules of civil procedure stipulate a procedure and time limit for every step of civil proceedings. A party who fails to comply with these requirements may be penalised. For example, if the defendant does not enter an appearance within 8 days after service of the writ, the plaintiff may apply for a judgment in

---

[141] *Id.*, r. 6.
[142] *Id.*, r. 9(1).
[143] For details of the powers of the Court of Appeal in determining an appeal, see *supra*, Chapter IV.A.2.b.
[144] *Id.*
[145] Ord. 57, r. 13(2); S.C.J.A., s. 37(3).
[146] Ord. 57, r. 15; S.C.J.A., s. 41.
[147] For the rules governing the procedure for appeals to the Privy Council, see Ord. 58.
[148] Ord. 58, r. 2.
[149] See e.g., S.C.R., Ord. 1, r. 2(5).

default of appearance. The R.S.C. also provides devices for shortening the proceedings where a plaintiff has a groundless action or where the defendant has no real defence. On the other hand, the rigidity of technical requirements may occasionally result in injustice, and therefore, the court is given residual power or discretion to waive certain incidents of non-compliance in order to do substantial justice in the case.[150] In these ways, the rules of civil procedure try to ensure that disputes brought to court are disposed of as expeditiously and fairly as possible.

2. Civil Procedure in the Subordinate Courts

Even before the promulgation of the new Subordinate Courts Rules in March 1986,[151] civil procedure in the subordinate courts was already similar to that in the High Court in many respects.[152] With the 1986 Rules, however, subordinate court civil procedure has been streamlined and now follows that in the High Court even more closely.

The following are some of the more significant changes wrought by the new S.C.R.[153]

(a) Under the previous system, all contentious proceedings in the subordinate courts had to be commenced by summons.[154] This system required lawyers and/or the parties in a civil suit to attend the "mentions" court at several stages before the trial of the case proper. It was a time-consuming and inconvenient process for all concerned, and in particular, the junior lawyers, since cases were mentioned in order of the lawyer's seniority at the Bar. The new system allows subordinate court litigants to file writs of summons just as in the High Court,[155] and does away with the "mentions" system because, in line with High Court procedure, the Rules prescribe what the parties need to do after the filing of the writ. This makes it unnecessary for

---

[150] See e.g., Ord. 92, r. 4; Ord. 2, r. 1(2).
[151] The S.C.R. 1986 repealed the S.C.R. 1970, and was brought into force on 1 March 1986 by No. S 60/86.
[152] For a general comparison of civil procedure in the High Court and the subordinate courts prior to the 1986 Rules, see J. Prakash, "Civil Practice in Singapore: A Comparison Outline of Procedure in (the) High Court and Subordinate Court(s)" in *Practice Law Manual: Vol. 3 — Procedure* (R.J. Ennis ed.), pp. 586-595 (Board of Legal Education Practice Law Course, July 1985).
[153] See *The Sunday Times*, March 2, 1986, p. 9.
[154] S.C.R. 1970. Ord. 4, r. 2.
[155] S.C.R. 1986, Ord. 5.

the parties to appear in court until the trial or unless they have certain applications to make.

(b) Previously, summary judgment was not available in the subordinate courts. However, the new Rules empower the Registrar to deliver summary judgment.

As in the High Court, these new features of subordinate court civil procedure are designed to save time, costs and labour.

Subordinate court judgments for the payment of money may be enforced in the same ways as High Court judgments, *i.e.*, by writ of seizure and sale, garnishee proceedings, a charging order, the appointment of a receiver, or an order of committal in appropriate cases.[156]

Appeals from the subordinate courts lie to the High Court exercising appellate civil jurisdiction.[157] The procedure is set out in the S.C.R.[158] A party dissatisfied with the judgment of the High Court may be able to appeal further to the Court of Appeal and then to the Privy Council.[159]

---

[156] *Id.*, Ord. 45.
[157] See *supra*, Chapter IV.A.2.a.(iii).
[158] Ord. 54.
[159] See *supra*, Chapter IV.A.1.

Chapter VI

Conclusion

It is appropriate to conclude this general survey of the Singapore legal system with some brief comments on legal culture, and future legal development.

A. Singapore Legal Culture[1]

In most countries, there is often a gap between the law in theory and the law in action.[2] This gap is a partial reflection of a country's legal culture.[3] L. Friedman defines "legal culture" to mean "the values and attitudes ... which determine the place of the legal system in the culture of the society as a whole ... the network of values and attitudes relating to law, which determine when and why and where people turn to the law, or to government, or turn away ... legal culture is the term we apply to those values in society which determine what structures are used and why; which rules work and which do not, and why."[4]

Thus, a more realistic account of the Singapore legal system should attempt to take into consideration the legal culture of Singapore as this would shed valuable light on how the Singapore legal system actually functions in practice. However, a detailed exposition of Singapore legal culture is beyond the scope of this work, not least of all because empirical studies on the topic have yet to be attempted.[5] Nevertheless, a few random general observations can be made which await empirical verification.

A tentative survey of Singapore legal culture suggests that although the formal Singapore legal system has much in common with that of England in terms of methodology, legal theory and substantive rules, it in fact operates in a very different social, economic, political and cultural context which results in some disparity between the law in

---

[1] For a more detailed account, see P.N. Pillai, *State Enterprise in Singapore: Legal Importation and Development* (1983), pp. 1-42, 207-220.
[2] See R.B. Schlesinger, *Comparative Law: Cases-Text-Materials* (4th ed. 1980), p. 325.
[3] *Id.*, pp. 323-326; Pillai, *supra*, n. 1 at p. 1.
[4] L. Friedman, "Legal Culture and Social Development" (1969) 4 Law and Society Review 29.
[5] Pillai, *supra*, n. 1 at p. 7.

Conclusion

action in Singapore and that in England. This observation is especially true of the colonial Singapore legal system.

As previously explained, British colonisation resulted in English law becoming the formal law of the land (although certain ethno-religious customary practices were tolerated in limited areas such as family law). In daily life, however, each of the ethnic communities was, in fact, governed primarily by its own customary or religious practices. This was the "living" law of the land[6] in nineteenth century Singapore. This impression is borne out by the following historical accounts of colonial Singapore society.

When the English first arrived in 1819, Singapore was sparsely inhabited by a small community of Malay fishermen and a few Chinese. Four months later, the population had exceeded 5,000, and it was mainly Chinese.[7] Immigrants continued to pour into Singapore as cultivators, traders, artisans, skilled workers and labourers, so that by the 1860s, the population numbered more than 80,000, with the Chinese making up 65 percent of the population. The Indians were the second largest community, followed by the Malays. The European community was the smallest, numbering 94 in 1827 and less than 500 in 1860.[8] However, it possessed a disproportionate measure of wealth and influence.[9] By the end of the nineteenth century, Singapore was the most cosmopolitan city in Asia. Nearly 75 percent of the population were Chinese, but there were also sizeable minorities of Malays, Sumatrans, Javanese, Bugis, Boyanese, Indians, Ceylonese, Arabs, Jews, Eurasians and Europeans.[10] Nineteenth century Singapore society was a cultural hotchpotch of immigrants and colonialists drawn together by their common pursuit of individual economic prosperity.[11] Most of these communities carried their own unique traditions and customs to the colony. Against this demographic and social backdrop, it is not surprising that, although English law was the formal law of the land, in reality, it rarely impinged on the daily lives of the vast majority of the people during the colonial era.

---

[6] See M. Friedman, "Some Reflections on the Development of the Legal Culture of Singapore" (1980) The Law Times (Singapore), p. 12.
[7] R.H. Hickling, "The Influence of the Chinese Upon Legislative History in Malaysia and Singapore" (1978) 20 Mal. L.R. 265 at 266.
[8] C.M. Turnbull, *A History of Singapore 1819-1975* (1977), pp. 36-38.
[9] C.M. Turnbull, *The Straits Settlements 1826-67* (1972), p. 23.
[10] Turnbull, *supra*, n. 8, at p. 97.
[11] Hickling, *supra*, n. 7, at p. 268.

For instance, as regards the Chinese community which has been the largest single community in Singapore since 1827,[12] Purcell wrote that although there were as many as 70,000 Chinese in Singapore in 1857, there was not a single European who understood their language.[13] This is a significant and revealing statement since such a language barrier would surely have effectively isolated the Chinese community from the reach of English law and administration. Purcell also described British policy towards the Chinese in Malaya as a transition from indirect to direct rule *i.e.*, "from rule by Chinese custom administered by Chinese headmen, to rule by English criminal law side by side with Chinese custom administered by British judges, ... to rule by the law of England, taking into account of Chinese custom."[14] This transition took place over a number of decades.

Another historian, Turnbull, wrote that "[t]hroughout the whole period of Indian rule in the Straits Settlements, the Chinese community stood apart from British administration"[15] and the British authorities were, in turn, reluctant to interfere with them.[16] One important reason why English law and administration were unable to penetrate the Chinese community lay in the fact that the Chinese community was governed by powerful secret societies which had been imported from China with the first immigrants.[17] These societies presented a serious obstacle to the British judicial system because their rules were often directly at odds with it.[18] For example, members were forbidden to submit their disputes to the courts, give evidence against fellow members or supply information to the authorities.[19] Disputes among Chinese were generally settled within the community according to its rules and customs.[20]

---

[12] Turnbull, *supra*, n. 8, at p. 36.
[13] V. Purcell, "Chinese in Malaya under the British, 1786-1874" in *Malaysia: Selected Historical Readings* (1966), compiled by J. Bastin and R.W. Winks, at p. 175.
[14] V. Purcell, *The Chinese in Malaya* (1948), p. 143.
[15] Turnbull, *supra*, n. 9, at p. 127.
[16] *Id.*
[17] Purcell, *supra*, n. 13.
[18] See Turnbull, *supra*, n. 9, at p. 123; L.A. Mills, *British Malaya 1824-67* (1961), p. 243.
[19] *Id.*
[20] See C.S. Wong, *A Gallery of Chinese Kapitans* (1964), p. 11, Turnbull, *supra*, n. 9, at pp. 106-107, 123.

Conclusion 133

From the foregoing, it may be seen that long after the colonial courts had affirmed that English law was the law of the land,[21] the various ethnic communities continued to be governed primarily by their own customs and traditions in daily life. Although this gap between the formal law and the real law has become narrower with the passage of time as the various immigrant communities gradually sank roots in Singapore and evolved into a new and more integrated society, vestiges of this dichotomy remain even today.

In the twentieth century, and particularly in the last twenty years or so, the trend has increasingly been towards legal integration.[22] The Women's Charter 1961, which unified family law for all ethno-religious groups except Muslims, is a good example of this movement towards legal integration. Other factors which have contributed towards legal integration include the erosion of traditional family and community ties and the increasingly important role of public law.[23] Cultural norms and English law are gradually being blended into a more homogenous legal system with a strong regulatory flavour.[24]

However, in spite of these changes, there are still some aspects of Singapore legal culture which remain largely unchanged. Most prominent of all is the traditional Confucian respect for law and authority among Singaporeans of Chinese descent who make up 76 percent of the population. It has been postulated that this particular aspect of the Singapore legal culture helps to account for the general law-abiding character of Singapore society and the general tolerance of (or even a preference for) a strong, paternalistic government. Traditional Chinese philosophy also helps to explain the general reluctance of the average Singaporean to invoke litigation as a mode of dispute settlement.[25] Chinese tradition frowns upon litigation as undesirable behaviour which disrupts social harmony.[26] Although these traditional attitudes are slowly changing (particularly among younger Singaporeans) as a result of westernisation, education and modernisation, their general prevalence even today helps to explain why the average

---

[21] In a series of cases dating from 1835, the colonial courts held that the Second Charter had introduced English law as it existed on 26 November 1826 into the colony: see R. Braddell, *The Law of the Straits Settlements* (3rd ed. 1982), p. 27.
[22] See Friedman, *supra*, n. 6.
[23] *Id.*, at p. 13.
[24] *Id.*
[25] Pillai, *supra*, n. 5.
[26] See S. van der Sprenkel, *Legal Institutions in Manchu China* (Rep. 1977), pp. 33, 76-79, 127, 135-136; R. David and J. Brierley, *Major Legal Systems in the World Today* (3rd ed. 1985), pp. 518-519.

Singaporean is not as conscious of his legal rights nor as litigious as his counterparts in other common law countries such as the U.S.A, England and India,[27] and especially in disputes involving government agencies.[28] Traditional informal modes of dispute settlement (*e.g.* mediation) are still much preferred.

The above information facilitates a better understanding of the actual role of the legal system in Singapore society. Such an understanding would not be possible if we look at the "book law" alone. For this reason, it is hoped that empirical studies on the legal culture of Singapore will be undertaken in the near future.

B. Future Legal Development

In Chapter I, it was seen that British colonisation was the phenomenon responsible for bringing the Singapore legal system into the common law fold. More specifically, the Singapore legal system joined the common law family because those entrusted with shaping its initial development were common lawyers. The essence of the common law system does not lie in rules of substantive law but in the unique methodology practised by common lawyers.[29] This is a peculiar mental attitude and habit of legal thought that historically evolved in England, but continues to be utilised by lawyers in all legal systems identified as belonging to the common law family today.[30] Thus, the common law tends to be carried wherever common lawyers go, and the reception of English common law by legislative fiat is generally preceded by the arrival of common lawyers. This has generally been the experience of the legal systems within the common law family today. English settlers or colonialists were responsible for the extension of the common law to those territories.[31]

The Singapore legal system remains a common law system today because it continues to be operated by common lawyers.[32] In this regard, it may be noted that a significant number of legal practition-

---

[27] Pillai, *supra*, n. 1 at p. 9.
[28] *Id.*, p. 10.
[29] G.W. Bartholomew, "The Singapore Legal System" in *Singapore: Society in Transition* (Riaz Hassan ed. 1976), p. 100.
[30] *Id.*
[31] For instance, long before the Federated Malay States received English law by statutory enactment, a general reception of English law had occurred because of the arrival of English-trained lawyers and judges: see Bartholomew, *supra*, n. 29 at p. 102.
[32] *Id.*

Conclusion

ers and judges in Singapore are English-trained.[33] Even locally-trained lawyers do not escape English legal influence because Singapore legal education is very much English-influenced in terms of courses, literature and teachers. Together with the continued retention of the Privy Council as court of last resort, these factors strongly contribute to the perpetuation of the English common law in Singapore.

However, history has shown that legal methodology can and does change with time,[34] and therefore, it is quite possible that the present legal *status quo* may change in the distant future. In fact, deviations from English law have already occurred in the realm of substantive law, particularly in non-commercial law areas such as social, criminal and economic legislation.[35]

A variety of factors have contributed to Singapore's divergent development in substantive law.

(a) As different needs and problems arose, Singapore law has had to develop to meet those needs. For example, the Civil Law (Amendment) Act 1979 was intended to restrict the "blanket" importation and application of English law, especially in view of the fact that British membership in the E.E.C. might develop English law in directions unsuited to Singapore.[36]

---

[33] As at March 1986, 26.8% of those admitted to the Singapore bar were English-trained; (Singapore) Law Society's Journal, Vol. 3 No. 1, March 1986, p. 1; and 7 out of the 8 Supreme Court judges had received their legal training in England, there being only 1 locally-trained Supreme Court judge.

[34] *Id.* See e.g., Schlesinger, *supra*, n. 2 at p. 304.

[35] For example, it may be noted that the criminal law and procedure of Singapore have long been closer to the Indian than the English position because they were originally borrowed in codified form from India in the nineteenth century. Recent developments in these areas of law appear to carry the Singapore legal system still further from the English model. See for example, the Misuse of Drugs Act 1973, No. 5 of 1973, Reprint 1978; the Penal Code (Amendment) Act 1984, No. 23 of 1984; the Criminal Procedure Code (Amendment No. 2) Act 1984, No. 24 of 1984; and the Arms Offences (Amendment) Act 1984, No. 25 of 1984. In introducing heavier penalties, minimum or mandatory sentences for certain types of offences, and tougher procedures, these pieces of legislation reflect the Singapore government's recent tougher attitude towards a growing crime rate. These measures were clearly addressed to the peculiar needs of Singapore society; see *e.g.* Singapore Parliamentary Debates Official Report, Vol. 44, cols. 1861-1883, 1897-1903. Examples of indigenous social and economic legislation are the Women's Charter, Reprint 1981 (Cap. 47) and the Industrial Relations Act, Cap. 122, respectively. See Pillai, *supra*, n. 1 at pp. 38-39.

[36] See Singapore Parliamentary Debates Official Report, Vol. 39, No. 7, 21 September 1979, cols. 445-448.

(b) There has also been an increasing output of statutes not modelled on English law or without English counterparts, particularly in the areas of social, criminal and economic legislation. The Misuse of Drugs Act 1973 is an example that springs readily to mind. This Act was uniquely tailored to meet peculiar Singapore needs and problems.[37] In interpreting and applying such statutes, Singapore judges have no choice but to develop the law independently.[38]

(c) Legal systems are rarely monolithic. In the course of their historical development, most of them imbibe influences from more than one quarter. This has been the Singapore experience as well. Thus, although the present Singapore legal system is a predominantly English common law one, Muslim and *adat* law remain relevant in family law matters. In addition, in the fields of criminal law and procedure, Singapore law is much closer to that of India than England. Singapore company law is also closer to the Australian than the English model. As the world grows smaller, the eclectic borrowing of laws and legal ideas has become an increasingly widespread practice. Singapore substantive law is likely to diverge further from the English model as it borrows increasingly from other sources as well. Future attempts at legal harmonisation within Asean (whose members come from very diverse legal backgrounds) are likely to compound this effect.[39]

The above factors will continue to contribute to divergent development in Singapore substantive law in the future. As regards common law development in particular, it is significant to note that the Privy Council itself has recently recognised that it is, in principle, possible for the common law to develop differently in different countries.[40] However, apart from the latest two Privy Council decisions on this point which appear to suggest that divergent development will prob-

---

[37] *Supra*, n. 35.
[38] This has generally been the American experience too: see generally, M. Rheinstein, "The United States of America" in *International Encyclopaedia of Comparative Law* (1976), Vol. I-U, pp. U-136, U-142-144; H.J. Berman, "The Historical Background of American Law" in *Talks on American Law* (Rev. ed. 1973), p. 11.
[39] For example, ASEAN member countries are in the process of either drafting or seriously studying laws on confiscating the illegally-acquired assets of drug traffickers: see *The Sunday Times*, 15 September 1985, p. 9.
[40] See *Australian Consolidated Press* v. *Uren* [1969] 1 A.C. 590; Lord Diplock, "Judicial Control of Government" [1979] 2 M.L.J. cxl at cxli; *Jamil bin Harun* v. *Yang Kamsiah* [1984] W.L.R. 668. *cf. de Lasala* v. *de Lasala* [1979] 2 All E.R. 1146 at 1153; *Hart* v. *O'Connor* [1985] 3 W.L.R. 214; *Tai Hing Cotton Mill Ltd.* v. *Liu Chong Hing Bank Ltd. and Ors* [1985] 2 W.L.R.. 317. See also *supra*, Chapter II.D.

Conclusion

ably not be sanctioned in the field of commercial law,[41] the precise boundaries of permissible independent common law development remain uncertain.[42] Be that as it may, countries like Singapore which still retain appeals to the Privy Council now have a measure of local autonomy (albeit limited) in developing their own brand of the common law.

Thus, although they share a common legal methodology, different needs and circumstances in Singapore and England will continue to propel the two countries along diverging paths of substantive law development in the future.

At present, however, the Singapore legal system remains firmly grounded in English law in terms of both methodology and important areas of substantive law such as mercantile law. Although there have been significant departures from the English model in the field of substantive law, these have been primarily in the areas of social, criminal and economic legislation. In spite of the 1979 amendment to section 5 of the Civil Law Act which set up a sluice-gate for tighter control of the reception of English mercantile law, English law still remains the foundation of Singapore mercantile law today.[43]

The above *status quo* is unlikely to change dramatically in the near future. In fact, it is likely to prevail for a long time to come. This observation may evoke the following question: is the Singapore legal system likely to become more autochthonous in the future?

This question may seem particularly pertinent in the light of interesting recent developments in the Malaysian legal system which has close historical links with the legal system of Singapore. In recent years, Bahasa Malaysia has been increasingly used in Malaysian courts. This is a significant break from the traditional position which permitted only English as the language of the courts. Another legal landmark occurred in 1985, when the Malaysian judiciary gained full judicial sovereignty with the total abolition of Privy Council appeals from Malaysia. Although these developments are unlikely to be followed in Singapore, their occurrence does raise the question

---

[41] See *supra*, n. 40, *Hart v. O'Connor* and *Tai Hing Cotton Mill Ltd.*
[42] See *supra*, Chapter II.D.
[43] See the comments of the Minister for Home Affairs at the second reading of the Bill, Singapore Parliamentary Debates Official Report, Vol. 39, No. 7, 21 September 1979, col. 447.

whether the Singapore legal system might develop more independently in the future.

The Singapore legal system is still in a state of transition because it is comparatively young. Although Singapore was colonised by the British more than 180 years ago, she has been independent from British rule for only 23 years (*i.e.*, since 1963), and has been a fully independent republic for only 21 years (i.e., since 1965). Judicial autonomy is still lacking in the sense that the Privy Council has been retained as the country's highest appellate court. Thus, it would be inappropriate to compare Singapore's legal development with that of many other common law countries which gained both political and judicial independence from English rule much earlier. Autochthony is essentially a product of time and circumstances. The U.S.A., for example, has enjoyed more than two centuries of political and judicial independence. Given different needs and conditions and the passage of time, it is not surprising that American law has developed a number of unique features and deviated from the English common law model[44] to the extent of being considered an alternative common law model.[45]

While the Singapore legal system has not diverged from the English model to the extent of the U.S.A., or even Malaysia, this does not mean that no indigenous legal development has taken place at all. Significant examples of indigenous substantive law (developed in response to the peculiar needs of Singapore society) are readily found particularly in the fields of social, criminal and economic legislation. Even in the realm of commercial law, the seeds of divergent development have already been sown by the 1979 amendment to section 5 of the Civil Law Act, which has given Singapore courts deciding mercantile issues wider powers to screen out English laws not suited to Singapore. It is possible that the peculiar needs and circumstances of Singapore society might, in future, result in legal innovations of an even more fundamental character. The passage of time and the process of evolution are likely to witness the progressive indigenization of the Singapore legal system.

---

[44] See generally, P.S. Reinsch, *English Common Law in the Early American Colonies* (1970); R.B. Morris, *Studies in the History of American Law* (2nd ed. 1959).
[45] Thus, the common law tradition is sometimes referred to as the Anglo-American common law tradition: see *e.g.* K. Zweigert and H. Kotz. *An Introduction to Comparative Law: Vol. 1— The Framework* (1977), p. 189; Rheinstein, *supra*, n. 38 at p. U-136.

INDEX

Administrative Law, 27
Attorney-General, 42, 94-96

Case Law, see Sources of Law, Judicial Precedents
Central Narcotics Bureau, see Law Enforcement Agencies
Civil Procedure, 119-129
  Appeals, 54-55, 61, 63-64, 126-129
  Enforcement of Judgments, 125-126, 129
  High Court, 120-128
    Post-trial, 125-128
    Pre-trial, 120-123
    Trial, 123-125
  Pleadings, 104, 121-123
  Rules of the Supreme Court, 119-120, 128
  Subordinate Court, 128-129
Commercial and Industrial Security Corporation, see Law Enforcement Agencies
Constitution, see Sources of Law
Corrupt Practices Investigation Bureau, see Law Enforcement Agencies
Courts, 49-79
  Coroners' Courts, 72-73
  Court of Appeal, 63-64
  Court of Criminal Appeal, 64-66
  District Courts, 66-70
  High Court, 58-63
  Juvenile Courts, 73-75
  Magistrates' Courts, 66-67, 70-72
  Privy Council, 4-5, 7, 9, 14-15, 50-55
  Shariah Court, 77-79
  Small Claims Tribunals, 75-77
  Subordinate Courts, 49, 66-77
  Supreme Court, 49, 55-66
    Appointment of Judges, 56-57
Criminal Procedure, 107-118
  Appeals, 55, 61-62, 64-66, 116-118
  Bail, 110, 118
  Post-trial, 116-118
  Pre-trial, 108-112
  Punishments, 116
  Rights of Accused, 107, 109-110

  To silence, 108, 111, 114
  Trial,
    High Court, 112, 115
    Summary, 112-115
Custom, see Sources of Law
Customs and Excise, see Law Enforcement Agencies
Customary Law, 8-11
  Malay, 10-11, 20, 39, 77-79
English East India Company, 1-2, 4-5, 11
English Law,
  Charters of Justice,
    First, 4-5, 8-9
    Second, 5-8, 13-14, 18
    Third, 5-6, 8-9
  Reception,
    General, 4-13
    Qualifications, 7-13
    Scope, 13
    Specific, 14-19
    Mercantile Law, 14-17
Executive, see Structure of Government

Imperial Acts, 11, 12, 23
Independence of the Judiciary, 57-58
Indian Legal Influence, 11-12, 19, 23, 39

Japanese Occupation, 3
Judicial Precedents, see Sources of Law
Judicial System, see Courts
Judiciary, see Courts, Structure of Government

Law Enforcement Agencies, 96-101
  CISCO, 97-98
  CNB, 98-99
  CPIB, 99-100
  Customs and Excise, 101
  Police, 96-97
  Prisons, 100-101
Legal Aid, 109-110
Legal Culture, 130-134
Legal Development,
  Future, 134-138
Legal History, 1-20
Legal Institutions, see Attorney-General,

Courts, Law Enforcement Agencies, Legal Profession, Legal Service
Legal Pluralism, 10-11, 19-20, 39, 77-79, 131-133
Legal Profession, 80-92
  Disciplinary Proceedings, 88-92
  Foreign Lawyers, 88
  History, 80-81
  Pupillage, 85
  Qualifications for Admission, 82-87
    Articled Clerks, 87
    Hong Kong Practitioners, 86-87
    Malayan Practitioners, 85-86
    "Qualified Persons", 83-85
Legal Service, 92-93
Legislation, see Sources of Law, Statutes
  By Reference, 14-18, 23
Legislative History, 11-13, 23
Legislative Process, 44-47
Legislature, see Structure of Government
Mercantile Law,
  Civil Law Act, s. 5, 14-19, 23
Muslim Law, 20, 77-79

Personal Law, see Customary Law
Political History, 1-4
Presidential Council for Minority Rights, 45-47
Privy Council, see Courts
Procedure, see Civil Procedure, Criminal Procedure

Comparison of Civil and Common Law Approaches, 102-107

Reception of English Law, see English Law

Sources of Law,
  Academic Writings, 40
  Constitution, 21-23
    Amendment, 22-23
    Supremacy, 21-22, 47-48
  Custom, 39-40
  Judicial Precedents, 28-39
    English, 34-39
    Stare Decisis, 28-34
  Statutes, 23-26
    Interpretation, 24-26
  Subsidiary Legislation, 26-27, 47-48
Statutes, see Sources of Law
Straits Settlements, 2-3, 5-12, 14, 19
Structure of Government,
  Executive, 41-42
  Judiciary, see also Courts, 48
  Legislature, 43-48
    Composition, 43-44
Subsidiary Legislation, see Sources of Law

Young Offenders, 73-75